Foreclosure Investing in the New Economy

A Distressed Property Investing Tutorial for New and Intermediate Real Estate Investors

Foreclosure Investing in the New Economy

A Distressed Property Investing Tutorial for New and Intermediate Real Estate Investors

KIRBY COCHRAN

overdue books

Mapleton, Utah

First Edition, June 2009 (20090625)

Library of Congress Control Number: 2009929439

ISBN-13: 978-1-887309-11-0

ISBN-10: 1-887309-11-X

Overdue Books LLC

Mapleton, Utah

http:/www.overduebooks.net

Acknowledgments

Chad Jardine, my close associate and friend, provided invaluable assistance as both editor and researcher for this book. His contribution was especially helpful in bringing the principles and practices of my real estate investing process to life in book form.

Contents

Introduction

Real estate investing is the ultimate mixed bag. Home ownership has been inseparable from the American Dream since the beginning. The rich all seem to understand the enduring value of real estate and their wealth always seems to contain significant real estate holdings. Historically, land ownership has almost been synonymous with wealth.

Yet, at the same time, a flood of infomercials and get-rich-quick personalities have preached real estate investing to the masses—and left scores of failures littered in their wake. Everyone seems to know someone who got rich in real estate and someone else who went broke.

How can people new to real estate investing hope to make sense of it all?

Like any investment process, participants become more competent with experience. The question is, can new investors afford the price to gain the necessary experience to generate investment returns?

A real and significant challenge for novice real estate investors is that real estate investing involves big transactions. Buying houses is not like collecting coins or opening an account on E*Trade. For example, stock market investors have the luxury of being able to invest almost any amount, large or small. They can effectively tailor their risk to losses they can afford (that is not to say that they always *do*).

With real estate, the ante is bigger. This means many players end up going all in on their first hand. Their first opportunity to gain experience requires all the capital they can muster—it takes everything they have got. If they survive, they go on to play again—if not, the tuition they paid to learn the ropes ends up being very high.

When I was a boy, one of my high school teachers told me, "The trick in life is to get wise before you get old." He meant that to the extent that I could watch, listen, and learn from the experiences of others, I would not have to pay the price to gain that experience myself.

That is what this book is all about. I want to give you the opportunity to learn from my experience without paying the *dumb tax* associated with making all of your own mistakes along the way.

Rather than throw you in at the deep end and watch you sink or swim through the various (and often very sophisticated) elements of the deal, or giving you instructions on a narrow and specific methodology that leave you helpless when the terms of a deal change in ways that a narrow methodology does not anticipate, instead, I will give you the building blocks—the tools that form a solid foundation to get you started.

I bought my first property in 1981 and have been involved in real estate development and investing for most of my life. I have done well, and I have been burned. As a result, my company has systematized and perfected many of the techniques I discuss here. When appropriate, I will add insights about the methodologies we have developed as well as the approaches typical for individual investors.

Now, I need to include a caveat. This book cannot buffer you entirely from the realities of the real estate market. No book can, and there is nothing that substitutes for gaining your own experience.

There is no guarantee that you will profit—no safety net other than your own understanding when it comes to investing in distressed property. It is up to you to build and grow your understanding of the market and learn the ropes in the market or region where you intend to do business.

There are not really any short-cuts and the last thing you want to do is become a foreclosure investor whose bad deals have you facing foreclosure yourself.

It *is* possible, however, to go through the process of gaining

> *The last thing you want to do is become a foreclosure investor who is facing foreclosure yourself*

that experience *prepared*. You can be prepared with tools and information that increase your probability of success. You can learn from my mistakes and successes to hopefully limit your exposure to your own missteps. I cannot guarantee that you will never get burned in a deal, but I can help you go into that deal with your eyes open.

FORECLOSURE INVESTING IN THE NEW ECONOMY

Distressed Real Estate Primer

FORECLOSURE INVESTING IN THE NEW ECONOMY

CHAPTER ONE

Real Estate Value

What makes real estate valuable? What is at the essential core of real estate ownership? Why is a piece of property, whether it is your house, or an apartment building, or a tract of land different than any other thing you can own? Why is it different than your car, your TV, or another possession? What makes it an *investment*? And, why is it even an investment worth considering?

The investment comes because, under normal circumstances, real estate appreciates in value, meaning it is worth more over time. This happens without any effort on the part of the property owner and happens on all types of real estate, from raw land to high-rise condos to commercial property.

Of course, not all types of property appreciate at the same rate, and any of them can go through periods where their value drops, but over the long-term, appreciation is a fact of life in the real estate market and is the basic mechanism behind real estate investing.

So, the question remains: *Why* do property values appreciate? What process is at work here? How does the appreciation mechanism operate?

The essential characteristic that drives real estate values is *uniqueness*. There is exactly one of any particular piece of property.

> **"The essential characteristic that drives real estate values is uniqueness"**

One piece of property may be like another, but it cannot be identical. If one piece of property could be *exactly similar* to another, real estate values would boil down to a simple function of square footage, amenities, age, and some objective measure of construction features and quality.

Instead, property in the foothills is more valuable than that in the valleys, property with a view is worth more than property that is obstructed or boxed in by other buildings. Properties with functionally similar construction and amenities can be worth drastically more based upon the precise parcel of land on which they are located.

How many times have you heard someone mention the three cardinal rules in real estate: Location, location, location? This cliché is striking at the central element that drives real estate values, which is the uniqueness of each property.

In this respect, real estate is like fine art. There is only one of each of Van Gogh's original oil paintings, and there is likewise only one of each particular property.

It is uniqueness that drives appreciation and appreciation underpins traditional real estate investing.

Think about it in terms of supply and demand. The supply of any particular property is always simply *one*. As the population grows, so does demand. Since supply is fixed, the equilibrium of supply and demand elevates price. In the next sections, I will discuss some of the manipulations of that model that have been at work in creating and bursting the housing bubble.

I mentioned that, notwithstanding the market forces driving appreciation, real estate can go through periods where properties drop in value. The current real estate climate is rife with distress where artificial manipulations have distorted the relationship between price and value. These distortions have caused time-tested market factors to become less reliable.

In fact, fluctuations in value are central to the operation of the distressed real estate market.

CHAPTER TWO

The Distressed Real Estate Market

Real estate professionals talk about the three D's that drive sales: *Death, divorce* and *distress*. Each of these conditions creates a *motivated seller*. A motivated seller is one for whom other considerations and objectives are more important than getting the best price from their real estate transaction. They need something else more than they need to get the highest possible price. Their level of motivation can be described in terms of what price below market value will be acceptable to them in light of whatever else it is that they need more.

Essentially, the value of the property to the seller *has become less* than it might be to potential buyers in the marketplace, often because one of the motivating factors, one of the three D's, is at work. Investors step in to take advantage of that motivation by negotiating a lower price than what might otherwise be considered *fair value*. Another description of fair value is the value of the property on the open market where the equilibrium of supply and demand determine price.

In essence, investors provide a vehicle for properties to move between hands where they are undervalued to hands where they are fair valued. Along the way, they hope to convert the value disparity between sellers and buyers into cash for themselves. As an investor in distressed real estate, you need to understand and be comfortable with your role in that process.

There are plenty of players in this business that are predatory—they sniff out motivated sellers like a shark smelling blood in the water. These characters abandon their values for a chance to make a quick buck.

Before you find yourself in a position that could compromise your integrity, it is a good idea to take stock of your values. I always say that your values in business are those things that you care about more than money.

By establishing what those values are before you venture out, you can avoid the ethical breaches and outright fraud that end up getting investors in the worst kind of trouble. If you hold on to those values, when a deal comes your way that has incredible upside potential, but requires you to cross the line, you will have the strength of character to walk away. Believe me, no deal is worth losing your self respect, your integrity, and possibly your freedom.

This is especially important because motivated sellers often have a lot to deal with. Remember the three D's, death, divorce, and distress?

The motivation for sellers that stems from death and divorce are straightforward. These are typically singular life-changing events, which clearly induce a circumstance where other concerns take priority over simply getting the most money out of the sale of a property. Distress, however, can be caused by many factors.

I need to make a quick clarification. *Distress* is sometimes used as a way of describing the *physical* condition of a property, meaning it is run down, dilapidated, or in bad repair.

For our purposes, however, we are looking at a property's *financial* condition. When we talk about distressed property, we mean property that is at some stage of *foreclosure*. Either it is at risk of foreclosure, is in the middle of foreclosure, or it has already been foreclosed on.

Typically property owners in financial distress are also experiencing a significant amount of emotional distress as well. They may be experiencing fear, anxiety, hostility, stress, trauma, denial, panic, anger, helplessness, and feel trapped and overwhelmed at their inability to resolve the problems that lead to their distress. You should not expect these property owners to act rational, thoughtful, or logical. They are often in a *fight or flight* state of mind, dealing with powerful emotions and anxiety. Human emotions are inseparable from the conditions that create the opportunity for investors. You may be thinking that a property in financial distress does not fit our definition of a motivated seller. You may think that *the property itself* in this scenario is not necessarily valued less by the seller—a borrower in financial distress. And if you ask the borrower, you will discover that they likely are still hopeful that they can save the property. They may be in denial about the severity of their financial condition, about their capacity to rectify it, and the necessity of selling their property at all. As far as they are concerned, the property is not for sale.

> *Foreclosure is the event that primarily indicates that this property is of interest to us*

In this case, the lower value is really more about the borrower's financial capacity to keep financial obligations current on the property. The emotional attachment and sentimental value represented, while not distinct in the mind of the property owner, *must* be separated from the strict financial valuation of the property in the mind of the investor.

Whatever the circumstances and economics that led the owner to default on the financing of the property, *foreclosure* is the event that primarily indicates that this property is of interest to us. The property may be in the early stages of distress, may only recently be in default, or may be further along in the process with foreclosure looming and imminent. Or foreclosure may have already taken place. In any case, the property ends up in the hands of a motivated seller, which creates an opportunity for investors.

Foreclosures have been around as long as lending and we can probably expect that a certain number of foreclosures will always exist. The current market (2009), however, is producing *historic numbers of foreclosures*, which also means we are entering a historic period of opportunity.

CHAPTER THREE

How We Got Here

The entire scope and ramifications of the housing crisis in this first decade of the new millennium is a topic that I expect will fill volumes and likely keep economists and historians busy for decades. Notwithstanding the enormity of the factors contributing to the state of the market, it is important for investors to have at least a basic historical context of how we got here.

What follows is a brief and intentionally truncated synopsis of the critical events leading up to the current state of affairs in real estate. (For a more thorough treatment of particular details leading up to the financial crisis, see *Anatomy of a Meltdown*, which can be viewed from my web site at *http://kirbycochran.com.*)

When the dot com bubble burst at the end of the 90's, investment money fled the stock market looking for safer havens. As a result, investment banks orchestrated instruments called Collateralized Mortgage Obligations (CMOs) that allowed investment money to be secured by real estate. This is the infamous *securitization* of mortgages that created the linchpin of many factors leading to the meltdown.

It made sense for investors to move to real estate. Historically, real estate in the U.S. had a stable long-term rate of appreciation (about 5.45 percent since the end of World War II).[1] Even though this was less than the historical average rate of return on Wall Street (7.8 percent), investors were prizing safety over aggressive returns after being badly burned by the tech stock reset.

These CMOs offered just what investors were looking for. The money that had fled Wall Street in the dot com crash, now came back into real estate securities like a tidal wave.

Not all of the mortgages backing the CMOs were created equal. Some of the mortgages were sub-prime— in other words these were loans given to borrowers with bad credit. Rating firms like S&P and Moodys issued the CMOs a credit rating, which theoretically took into consideration that sub-prime mortgages were riskier than typical *conforming* mortgages. The ratings were supposed to give investors the full picture of how one CMO compared with another in terms of risk. Now investors could not only invest in an instrument backed by real estate, but if they were looking for a little better return (paired of course with higher risk) they could invest where the credit rating was lower indicating higher risk. Stock market investors were used to protecting themselves against risky investments through diversification—they would spread their investments around in case one went bad—and they did the same thing with their investment in CMOs.

The effect of all this new investment in real estate was an insatiable demand for mortgages, *whether the borrowers had good credit or bad.* In response to the demand, lenders loosened their lending criteria in order to get more mortgages into the pool. They began offering *creative* financing, acquiring borrowers that would otherwise not qualify for a mortgage through ARMs, balloon mortgages, interest-only loans, and stated income or *liar* loans, all of which made mortgages easier to get for people with bad credit.

Borrowers were getting into homes they never could afford. Mortgage brokers pushed ethical limits in their efforts to drive up the loan volume through their brokerages in what has since become known as *predatory lending.* Cookie cutter luxury homes became so common the media began referring to them as McMansions.[2]

Since practically anyone could buy a home above their price range, demand on the overall housing market skyrocketed, and prices started to climb aggressively; contractors started building new homes as fast as they could—and all of it was based on a lie.

Homes were not really worth what people were paying, construction was not really worth what contractors were charging, borrowers were not really able to repay the mortgages they took out and the credit ratings did not truly reflect the risk of these investments.

In fact, the market manipulations had created a condition—a perfect storm—for overvaluation and *depreciation*.

In 2008, we saw the market start to unravel. The Federal Reserve had been raising interest rates to try and stop the runaway train of borrowing. In a policy bordering on irresponsible, the Fed raised interest rates 17 times consecutively and the market did not see a rate reduction for a period of 38 months. As a result, the ARMs started growing with climbing interest rates, the balloons started to mature, and the borrowers stopped being able to make their house payments.

An avalanche of foreclosures began to hit the market as these mostly sub-prime loans failed one after another. The predictable disaster started gaining momentum and the news started discussing the *housing bubble* and the *sub-prime mortgage crisis*.

In March of 2008, Bear Stearns—one of the five largest investment banks on Wall Street—imploded because of its heavy investment in CMOs, only to be followed in the autumn by Lehman Brothers Holdings, Merrill Lynch, and Morgan Stanley. Goldman Sachs, the lone survivor held on propped up by Berkshire Hathaway and the U.S. government, but it was not the same. Investment banking as an industry crashed and burned and virtually ceased to exist. The big five were then accompanied by other smaller banks and traditional financial institutions whose money was tied up in mortgages or mortgage backed securities.

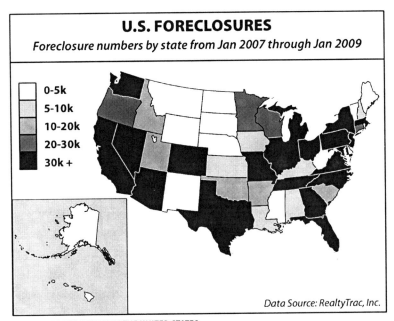

U.S. FORECLOSURES

Foreclosure numbers by state from Jan 2007 through Jan 2009

0-5k
5-10k
10-20k
20-30k
30k +

Data Source: RealtyTrac, Inc.

Figure 1: FORECLOSURES IN THE UNITED STATES

The effects were exacerbated by *leverage*, the term used for the ratio of dollars lent versus dollars held in deposit. Traditional banks were leveraged at a five to one ratio. In other words, for every dollar they had on deposit, they could loan five. Which meant that every dollar tied up in a foreclosure prevented five dollars from being loaned out.

Yet, that was nothing compared with the Wall Street firms. Investment banks like Lehman Brothers Holdings were leveraged as much as *35 to one*. This was the essential connection between foreclosures and the *credit crunch* which resulted as fearful banks halted lending and inter-bank borrowing, which froze money that had previously

15

been liquid and flowing through the economic system, in order to protect themselves. The Lehman Brothers leverage ratio effectively made it so $2 billion in foreclosures would *feel* like $70 billion!

With home values inflated by artificial demand, many borrowers were upside down—owing more on their homes than they were worth—making it impossible to refinance or sell.

> **Foreclosures are an essential and necessary part of the housing reset**

Borrowers with bad credit often had bought according to the *creative financing* terms pushed by their mortgage brokers, which meant that they got into their homes with little or nothing down and had virtually no *skin* in the game. Just when they couldn't afford to stay in their homes, it had never been easier to walk away from a mortgage—and so they did.

The current market is going through a painful period of *deleveraging*—also called a *reset* where the market should eventually return to price and value equilibrium. As much as foreclosures are lamentable—few financial failures are as painful as losing a home—*foreclosures are an essential and necessary part of that reset.*

Even with government and private support, credit is still tighter than it was. But, who can expect or desire lenders to return to the irresponsible lending they were doing?

The market is contracting because it needs to return to the point that buyers can buy what they can afford. The only way for that to happen is for foreclosures to reset the portion of the market that is most out of line.

It is not just foreclosures, however, that will reset the market. By themselves, foreclosures cannot be the solution because foreclosures *alone* do not get the market back on track. Foreclosures just return properties to the banks, and banks are not in the real estate sales business. They want to loan money, but are prevented from doing so when their money is tied up in a *non-performing* asset, like a house with a mortgage that nobody is paying.

Banks do not look at property based on its market value: They look at it based on the money they are losing by not having those dollars generating interest somewhere. That is why they are motivated sellers. They want to get the bad stuff off their books and get on to making money the way they know how.

So what is still needed in order to get the market going again? And where is the opportunity for an investor to enter the distressed real estate picture and create value for the parties involved and make some money? That is where real estate investors come in.

CHAPTER FOUR

The Opportunity in Distressed Real Estate

Properties which have been repossessed by the bank are called Real Estate Owned, or REO, properties. Bulging REOs on bank balance sheets will not reset housing prices to their intrinsic value.

The solution to getting the market back on track, where prices and intrinsic value are paired, requires *someone* to match foreclosures with new buyers. Someone has to get properties away from the banks and into the market.

In other words, the reset means that properties need to go from their inflated rates, to fair market value.

But the pendulum cannot simply swing from *overvalued* to *fair valued*. It has to *overcorrect* in order to get participation from those with the expertise to facilitate the transition. In other words, investors like you and me need to be able to make some money for our efforts in moving property from the hands of the banks into a reset fair-valued marketplace.

Where is the overcorrection going to come from?

Motivation exists for sellers in every stage of the foreclosure process. Property owners in default are motivated and may be capable of selling their property low enough that there is a margin available for investors. Beyond that, investors are looking at the lender as a motivated seller. Being motivated means the bank has a reason to accept a lower price than fair market value (in spite of whatever they might tell you).

They have many criteria for deciding what price they are willing to accept. They are asking questions like: How much is left owing on the mortgage? What is the cost of having those dollars tied up in the property? What is our reasonable expectation for the property, in other words, how much do we think we could get out in the marketplace?

In today's catastrophic economy, often banks are willing to sell their REO pools for 80, 65, 50 cents on the dollar or less. That margin represents work that bankers are unwilling or unable to do. Bankers are not real estate professionals. They are not contractors. To them, property represents *inventory*—it is like shelves of unsold goods.

Where a good Realtor® might talk to a buyer about a home's potential, the merits of the local schools or the realization of lifelong dreams, bankers do not think like that. They do not see the emotional component of selling someone their dream home, or selling an investment that might mean a secure retirement. Bankers live by the numbers, and as such, are terribly equipped to get good value out of these properties.

On top of the lender's lack of appreciation for the emotional dimension of selling, add the fact that these properties are often in very poor condition, often due to borrowers being upset that the bank decided to foreclose, or being embarrassed that they have been kicked out of their home.

In any case, they often stop being interested in basic maintenance and upkeep of the property. Sometimes borrowers intentionally take out their frustrations on the home. It is not uncommon to see things like concrete poured down toilets, dwellings left open to be ransacked and vandalized by local gangs, and everything of possible value stripped out from appliances to copper pipes. These homes cease to function according to the economics of the general market because, even though emotions don't matter to banks, they do to buyers.

A home that has every descriptive field filled in on a Realtor's profile could be listed for months without interest from potential buyers because of emotional factors that cannot be adequately described in such a profile.

If the property is an apartment building or a rental home, the complications can be even worse as worried and confused tenants try to figure out where they stand in the whole mess.[3]

In fact, dilapidated properties often become an issue for other community residents who resent eyesores in their neighborhood.[4] This is understandable. The neighbors are also victims of the market and are only trying to salvage what property value they have left.

Remember that to lenders, these properties are just inventory. They are not thinking about watering and mowing lawns, keeping algae from growing in the swimming pool, or keeping the property lit at night. These represent costs that lenders are loath to incur. As a result, some communities have started passing new laws requiring banks to pay for the upkeep of properties they own—all of which simply adds more financial pressure for banks to sell.[5]

These market factors and motivation for banks to sell are what creates the opportunity for savvy investors to buy real estate at less than its fair market value—sometimes *far* less—add value by cleaning, making repairs, remodeling, or simply making use of better sales and marketing tactics, and finally sell the property for more than their total cost.

Because banks operate more by the numbers, rather than soft factors. They often do not know whether the price they set is a good value or not. They typically hire a Realtor for a small fee to create a Broker's Price Opinion (BPO). BPOs often do not accurately reflect the price properties could bring in the market either. Lenders are looking at the implication on their own finances. They consider what it costs them to retain this property versus the potential loss they take by selling it cheap.

Now a word of caution: Just because you now understand the rationale behind why banks make motivated sellers, don't fall into the trap of thinking that bankers are foolish. They are typically very smart, especially when it comes to making money; they are just operating from a different perspective.

Because of this, you cannot count on the banker's price to tell you *anything* about the property's true value. And that means you need to go in with a system for estimating what the real value is. And that's where I can help.

The story of buying a home on the cheap, cleaning and fixing it up with your own labor and selling it to the market for a killing is a little bit of a fairy tale. Is there money to be made? Absolutely. Is it as easy as it sounds? Absolutely not. If it were that easy, everybody would be doing it.

There also seem to be dozens of get-rich-quick schemes built around investing in foreclosures. These schemes are really nothing more than a distraction to legitimate investors. There is a lot of risk in real estate investing and many people lose out, especially if they are unprepared. This book is about putting the probability of success in your favor.

It is certainly possible to be successful, especially if you are determined and ready to put in the work required—and from here forward, I will walk you through the steps to get prepared for your foray into the distressed property investing world, and the steps to take once you get there from start to finish.

Preparation

CHAPTER FIVE

Understanding the Playing Field

Finding distressed property is like playing football. Imagine you are covering receivers on defense and what you really want to get is an interception. The quarterback has the ball and is under pressure to pass it. If he does not get rid of the ball, he's going to get sacked.

The ball represents the property, of course. I use this metaphor to illustrate that, in order for you to intercept the ball, you need to know some things about it and about the game you are playing. You need to know whose hands it is in (who owns it), and the trajectory it will travel (the process) as the owner tries to pass it. And you need to know the rules surrounding how you can move in and grab it.

Figure 2 on the following page outlines the foreclosure process. I recommend that you take some time and get to know and understand each part of this illustration. This is like learning the playbook. When you can draw this out on your own and describe each element, you have a good foundation for understanding the more detailed and complex aspects of distressed property investing.

Don't worry. I'm going to go through it in detail in this section and will often refer back to it in later sections of this book.

As you can see along the right side of Figure 2, the process of foreclosure is broken down to three distinct stages: Pre-foreclosure, auction, and REO.

Each of these stages offers investors a chance to pick up properties at below market value, but the process for making the purchase is different for each one. The last section described the process from the borrower's point of new. Here I'm going to discuss what that means for you as an investor and some pros and cons about investing at each stage.

First, properties do not start out in distress. The potential for foreclosure lurks inside a purchase agreement that appears to be simply a mutually beneficial transaction. In the beginning, this agreement is formed between two entities: A borrower who wants to purchase a property and a bank who wants to make loans. The bank provides the funds the borrower needs to purchase the property. In return, the borrower promises to repay the bank what was borrowed, plus interest. The borrower's agreement to repay

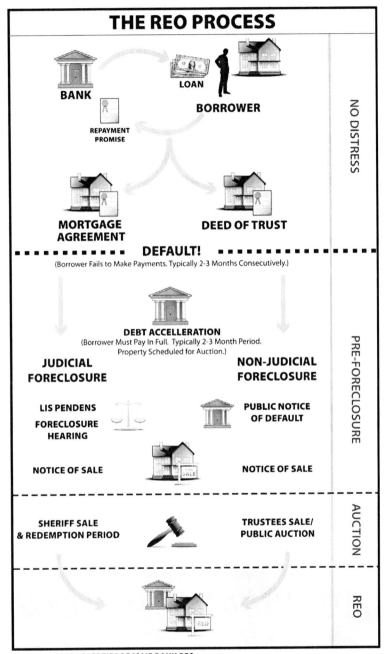

THE REO PROCESS

BANK

LOAN

BORROWER

REPAYMENT PROMISE

MORTGAGE AGREEMENT

DEED OF TRUST

NO DISTRESS

▪ ▪ ▪ ▪ ▪ ▪ ▪ ▪ ▪ ▪ ▪ **DEFAULT!** ▪ ▪ ▪ ▪ ▪ ▪ ▪ ▪ ▪ ▪ ▪ ▪ ▪

(Borrower Fails to Make Payments. Typically 2-3 Months Consecutively.)

DEBT ACCELLERATION
(Borrower Must Pay In Full. Typically 2-3 Month Period.
Property Scheduled for Auction.)

JUDICIAL FORECLOSURE

NON-JUDICIAL FORECLOSURE

LIS PENDENS

PUBLIC NOTICE OF DEFAULT

FORECLOSURE HEARING

NOTICE OF SALE

NOTICE OF SALE

PRE-FORECLOSURE

SHERIFF SALE & REDEMPTION PERIOD

TRUSTEES SALE/ PUBLIC AUCTION

AUCTION

REO

Figure 2: HOW PROPERTIES BECOME BANK REO

29

is a promissory note written into a contract memorializing the terms of the transaction.

The instrument that sets out the terms of this arrangement between banks and borrowers is generally either a mortgage agreement or a deed of trust (which one generally depends upon state laws and whether or not your state allows *non-judicial* foreclosures). Unless I am drawing a specific distinction, I will use the term *mortgage* to mean both mortgage agreements and deeds of trust since they effectively serve the same purpose: An agreement between the borrower and the lender.

The difference essentially boils down to how states administer property rights. At the most basic level, property rights in the U.S. are made possible because the government bears the responsibility for defending everything within its borders. In other words, all the property within the United States is subject to the laws of the United States and not some other country or regime because the United States defends its claim to that property by force of arms. That protection secures property rights under the law within the country and much of the administration of those rights falls to the states.

In states that use mortgage agreements, the states effectively assign the ownership of the property to the buyer. The lender's rights under the mortgage agreement contract must be pursued like any other contract dispute—through the courts.

Foreclosure in states that use a mortgage agreement, and therefore are processed through the courts, are called *judicial foreclosures*. Judicial foreclosures typically take longer than non-judicial ones.

Lenders, at the mercy of backlogged courts and legal expenses and headaches, promoted the idea of non-judicial foreclosure. Non-judicial foreclosure has been adopted by about 25 states. In a non-judicial foreclosure state, mortgages are executed using deeds of trust. With a deed of trust, a third party *trustee* actually owns the property and rights are granted to the borrower and lender by the contract.

Non-judicial foreclosure proceedings are handled by any *Power of Sale* terms in the mortgage as well as being governed by state law. Non-judicial foreclosures are generally handled outside the court system and can move much faster, saving carrying costs and time delays for the lender. Both types of foreclosure go through similar steps. I will outline the major distinctions that you should learn and understand as you embark on a career of distressed property investing.

Mortgage agreements in judicial foreclosure states typically use language identifying the borrower as the *mortgagor* and the lender as the *mortgagee*.

Deeds of trust in non-judicial foreclosure states, on the other hand, typically use language identifying the borrower as the *trustor*, and the lender as the *beneficiary*, and also name the third-party *trustee* who is neutral and holds the deed of trust.

The process of foreclosure, notices, timing, steps and requirements, is articulated in the terms of the mortgage contract (and, of course, by state law, but typically banks are very familiar with these laws and draft mortgage agreements in strict accordance with them.)

It is important to understand that foreclosure is not a single event, but rather a process. In Figure 2, you can see that the first phase of foreclosure is *Pre-Foreclosure* and the first step in pre-foreclosure is *Default*. Mortgage agreements will spell out the terms under which the loan is repaid and what constitutes default.

The most common type of default is failing to make scheduled payments. It is not unusual for mortgage agreements to include additional default provisions, such as if the buyer stores illegal hazardous wastes on the property or destroys the property in some way, but these provisions are really just a way for lenders to protect themselves from the rare and crazy things that could potentially put their stake in the property at risk. Generally speaking, missing payments is the most common way in which borrowers default on their promise under the mortgage contract.

There is some discretion on the part of the lenders about whether or not they exercise their rights to foreclose and when. Default could be viewed as placing the ball in the lender's court. The borrower has failed to meet obligations under the contract, and as a result, options are now open to the bank to protect itself. For example, banks do not usually initiate foreclosure after a single missed payment, but they may have the right to.

Depending on whether the mortgage is a mortgage agreement or a deed of trust, the bank will initiate judicial or non-judicial foreclosure.

Typically foreclosure starts after not merely default, but after two or three payments that have been missed consecutively. In times past, it has been a more reliable rule to say that banks would begin foreclosure 91 days after default. However, in our current market where foreclosures are high, banks have been known to allow borrowers to miss their payments for six months or more in order to avoid the necessity of foreclosure.

Banks may also choose to implement a workout agreement or a *forbearance*. These are temporary short-term agreements between borrowers and lenders that create new, short-term payment structures or adjustments to the original mortgage.

You should note that there are rarely any notices or public records indicating that such an agreement is in place between the borrower and the lender. Not knowing about these arrangements puts you at a disadvantage when it comes to negotiation, but you will be in the dark about it unless the borrower or the bank discloses it to you. In other words, you may want to ask about it directly and include it in any checklists you use when introducing yourself to borrowers in distress.

These workout agreements can be used to help borrowers catch up on payments and stay in the property in order to avoid the costly foreclosure process. If a bank believes that it can reasonably work with a borrower and cure the default, it has significant incentive to do so. One source claims that banks typically lose $50,000 on every home that goes into foreclosure.[6]

However, when the bank has had enough with the borrower in default, they often become convinced that the best way to protect themselves is to move ahead with foreclosure. At this point, the bank will exercise its right to *accelerate* the debt. This means that they notify the borrower that the *entire balance* of the loan must be repaid in a short period of time. The time in which the borrower can pay off the loan is called the *Reinstatement Period*.

At this point, the bank will also notify the borrower of the auction schedule. The Reinstatement Period typically runs up to five days prior to the auction date, which can be 2-3 months from the notice date.

Borrowers can try to sell the property during this period or pay the loan off with other funds. However, this is often a very high and difficult hurdle for borrowers to meet—especially considering that they were struggling just to make their monthly payments. Sometimes lenders will allow a loan to be reinstated if the default is corrected, that is, if the loan is merely brought current, rather than requiring the entire outstanding balance. But often the bank has exhausted its options for mending the relationship with the borrower. In that case, the bank may have made up its mind that foreclosure is the best course of action and the borrower is then subject to whatever terms in the mortgage contract govern the process of foreclosure.

Judicial foreclosures typically require the lender to file a lawsuit in order to get the property auctioned at a sheriff's sale. This process generally starts with the filing of a *lis pendens* (a notice of a claim of interest in the property and that a legal proceeding is determining the outcome of the claim.) A *lis pendens* will encumber the title of the property and anyone performing a title search will see it as a cloud. Typically, a *lis pendens* means that the ownership of all or part of a property is in dispute and that the dispute is part of a lawsuit; in this case, the lawsuit is that filed by the lender in order to exercise its right to foreclose.

After the *lis pendens* is filed, a foreclosure hearing is scheduled and held by the court. The judge will typically either throw out the case or order that the foreclosure proceeds.

No hearing before the court is required for non-judicial foreclosures, but a similar Notice of Default (NOD) is filed by the trustee with the county recorder's office. (Note, sometimes the county recorder is called the *register of deeds*.) Notice that it is the third-party trustee who files this notice on behalf of the lender.

The bank then files a Notice of Sale with the county and publishes the same in the appropriate local newspaper. You should check the area in which you are planning to invest in order to determine which newspaper is recognized as the one appropriate for posting of legal notices.

Getting information about properties at this stage is as simple as intercepting the property at some point in its process. During all of the aforementioned steps—everything between default and the foreclosure auction—the property is considered to be in pre-foreclosure, which means that the owner is a buyer in trouble, but typically still occupies and holds ownership rights to the property.

If you want to acquire a property at this stage of the process, you will be dealing with both the borrower who is losing his or her home as well as a bank who is not getting paid. Before jumping into this type of situation, you need to objectively ask yourself if you have the temperament to insert yourself into a thorny, temperamental and irrational relationship between these two.

If pre-foreclosures are your target, the notices and filings required to start foreclosure provide clues for you to move in and intercept.

CHAPTER SIX

Pre-Foreclosures

Pre-foreclosures generally involve the greatest number of parties, because even though the property is in distress, the lender has not actually completed the process of exercising its foreclosure and repossession rights.

As I mentioned earlier, that means that dealing with these properties requires dealing not only with lenders, but with borrowers in distress. You will need to be skilled and tactful in order to strike a deal under these conditions. Borrowers may be embarrassed, hopeful they can resolve the delinquency on their own, or hostile toward the lender or anyone else proposing a solution that requires them to leave the home. They may be very uncooperative and volatile.

You will need to be sensitive to the emotionally charged nature of negotiations under these conditions. I recommend you take a moment to ask yourself if you are honestly the type of person who can keep a cool head and de-escalate a borrower who may have every reason to be irrational, resentful and unpredictable.

Investors who favor buying pre-foreclosure properties often feel that buying during this stage helps them preserve profit margins that can be eroded during the competitive bidding of a public foreclosure auction, or likewise eroded as lenders incur additional legal and other costs involved in completing the foreclosure process.

Buying during pre-foreclosure may provide some other benefits to you as an investor. For instance, a cooperative homeowner may allow you to make a thorough inspection and estimate repairs and rehabilitation costs, whereas a property purchased at auction makes no provision for you to inspect prior to purchase.

When compared with bank-owned REO properties, pre-foreclosure investors tend to find banks rigid, cold and difficult to negotiate with. Bank-owned properties are often listed through real estate brokers who try to sell as high as possible. If utilities have been shut off, there is some risk that your ability to thoroughly inspect will be curtailed. And REO contracts are typically closed *as-is* just like auction properties (more about auctioned properties in Chapter 8, "Auctions").

Pre-foreclosure investors contend that the chances of purchasing a property at a significant discount to market value are best during the pre-foreclosure stage of the foreclosure process.

A word of caution about your risks with pre-foreclosure properties when a mortgage has a Due on Sale clause: Typically, your negotiation on a property in pre-foreclosure involves borrowers *and* lenders.

Is this always the case? Does it have to be? Why not simply negotiate the sale with the borrower, cure the default and assume the relationship with the lender?

There is a very good reason that you want to include the lender in your negotiations. It is the Due on Sale clause written in to most mortgage contracts. This clause is sometimes written in language like, "transfer of the property" or "transfer of a beneficial interest in borrower" and means that the lender may have the right to *call* the loan if the borrower sells the property.

Here's a potential scenario. You successfully negotiate with the borrower and execute a purchase contract. Of course since you are doing this without including the lender, your contract includes a provision that you are taking title to the property *subject to existing loans*. No borrower is going to sell you his house and still be on the hook for the mortgage payment.

Once you close the sale (in order to protect your investment), you immediately take out insurance on the property —and your insurance company dutifully notifies the lender that the property is insured—in *your* name.

The lender has now been tipped off that it has now become the mortgagee on a property that has changed ownership. It invokes the *Due on Sale* clause in its contract and calls the loan. In other words, the lender demands that the *entire loan* be paid within 30 days. If you are unable to come up with the cash, you are technically in default and now the foreclosure process has started anew, with *you* as the borrower.

In a scenario where you bought the borrower's interest by paying something near the amount of the borrower's equity in the property, and assuming that the loan is a much larger amount, you have just been hit with an expense for which you are woefully unprepared.

You can avoid this scenario in two ways. First, engage the services of a competent real estate attorney to review the borrower's mortgage contract and establish that there is no Due on Sale clause. Second, include the lender in your negotiations. As a rule, I always recommend the second approach.

CHAPTER SEVEN

Short Sales

What is a short sale? Short sale is the abbreviated form of *short payoff sale*, and includes those sales in which the lender who services the loan and the investor who owns the loan (typically a player in the secondary mortgage market like Fannie Mae or Freddie Mac) agrees to allow the borrower to sell the property for less than is owing on the mortgage.

Typically, this involves convincing the lender that the borrower is incapable of curing his default and that the property itself does not have a market value adequate to cover the loan value in a sale. Justifying a low price can involve data about the real estate market, the condition of the property, or other adverse circumstances.

Short sales are typically negotiated through the lender's loan loss mitigation department. In order for investors to discuss a short sale on behalf of a borrower, they must have received a written authorization from the borrower to disclose information about the loan. Otherwise the lender is bound by its obligation to protect the privacy of the borrower.

In years past, loan loss mitigation departments had what they called a *hardship test* which was criteria borrowers had to meet in order to be considered for approval of a short sale.[7] These criteria went above and beyond the basic economics of whether the property has any chance of bringing enough at sale to pay off the loan. They included such things as: Catastrophic illness or disability, death or death of a spouse, divorce, job loss or a job transfer that impacts the ability to dispose of the property, bankruptcy, military call to service or incarceration. Short sales pose some risks to the homeowners as well as to potential investors. In our current climate with high volumes of distressed property, banks are struggling and overwhelmed. Their portfolios of distressed non-performing assets have swollen to the point that they are impossibly unwieldy.

Time is of the essence in short sale transactions and some states require that any sales contracts made with homeowners facing foreclosure include a right of rescission clause, which allows homeowners some time to back out of the deal even after the contract is signed. Make sure you understand and follow the law in your state.

Speaking of timing, making an offer to sell short does not itself do anything to avoid or delay the process of foreclosure that has already begun. There is no automatic grace period extended by banks once a short sale offer comes in.

What that means is that a short sale offer could sit in an overwhelmed bank employee's inbox while foreclosure proceeds as normal. It is entirely possible that the property will go to public foreclosure auction before anyone with the lender has even had a chance to consider your offer. (REOs on the other hand have nowhere else to go. They are already at the end-of-the line in terms of the foreclosure process.)

Whereas a completed foreclosure wipes out all subordinate liens (more on liens in Chapter 22, "Liens") and mortgages, a short sale does not. The potential exists for the lender on a second mortgage who was not paid in full under the terms of your short sale, to come after and sue the previous homeowner to enforce its rights of repayment for the unpaid balance. When successful, these lawsuits typically yield a *deficiency judgment* against the previous homeowner.

> *It is entirely possible that the property will go to auction before anyone has had a chance to consider your offer*

At this point, you had better hope that you did not tell the homeowner anything that could be construed as legal advice regarding the risks of completing your short sale transaction, or the liability could extend to you as well.

Your best bet is to take on subordinate liens head on. Contact the lien holders, explain the imminence of foreclosure and the consequences of foreclosure to their lien (ie. that it will be wiped out). Offer to buy them out at a discount. I start at a discount of around 60 percent.

Short sales may also require that you deal with liens that are wrongful or fraudulent. This typically requires that you contest them in court.

A growing trend is for first and second mortgage lenders to agree to short sales part way. In other words, they agree to the short sale, but only with the provision of a promissory note that grants them the right to pursue previous homeowners for some of the deficiency at a later time.[8] Even though it is implied that lenders will not take advantage of this provision, no-strings attached short sales are becoming much less common.

Short sales also have some negative tax implications for the borrower. First, lenders typically do not allow the borrower to pocket any money in a short sale. So, the borrower is only allowed to escape his obligations on the debt—not to make any money. The debt cancellation, however, can be subject to income taxes[9] as ordinary income. In other words, the IRS looks at the amount of the debt that was written off by the lender as money earned by the short seller. You may want to consult your accountant regarding the impact of *debt-discharge income.*

In a scenario where the borrower sells short a home that was originally purchased for less that the short sale (but ostensibly has withdrawn the equity through successive mortgages), the borrower will show a tax gain of the difference.

The tax basis is equal to the original purchase price, plus improvements and less any depreciation and/or write-offs.[10] Federal tax laws may make this gain excludable under the home-sale-gain, but states may not.

Also, losses on a principal residence are not deductible, so the tax advantage of taking a loss is not available with a short sale.

CHAPTER EIGHT

Auctions

Pre-foreclosure encompasses all the steps necessary to take the property to auction. Because it is so pivotal, *Auction* is its own phase in the foreclosure process. Again there are subtle differences between judicial foreclosure and non-judicial foreclosure when it comes to auction requirements. Sometimes I will reference a public foreclosure auction, which means the same stage whether in a judicial foreclosure or a non-judicial foreclosure. Let's look at some of the particular differences between the two. Judicial foreclosures culminate in a sheriff's sale. These are the public foreclosure auctions that are physically held right on the courthouse steps.

Non-judicial foreclosures also culminate in a public foreclosure auction, but it is typically held by a private auction house and is called a public auction or trustees sale. These auctions are opportunities to bid on and purchase foreclosed properties.

The opportunity to purchase a property at less than market value is strongest in cases where the owner of the property had built up substantial equity in the property and the lender's cost elements factored into the opening bid allow the auction to start at well below market value. Our current climate of upside-down mortgages and high leverage by borrowers make public foreclosure auctions like this less likely than either pre-foreclosure or REOs to make a good investment. However, just because current trends are moving that direction doesn't mean that you won't find a great deal at a public foreclosure auction—it just means that as you begin looking for deals you want to try and stack probability in your favor and to do that you need to be aware of the trends.

Public foreclosure auctions also carry some risks that are typically not present in the same fashion as properties in either the pre-foreclosure stage or the REO stage of foreclosure.

For instance, sales are *as-is* combined with the fact that typically buyers do not get the opportunity to get inside and inspect these properties prior to auction. *As-is* means exactly what it says—the sale is final and non-recourse. There is no buyer's remorse grace period. There is no recourse based on the lack of seller's disclosures or hidden detriments within the property. There is no room for negotiation on the terms of the purchase. The flexibility you might have with a traditional seller to win concessions due to needed repairs, property features that could be liabilities, or financing peculiarities, do not exist with properties bought at auction. Terms are set in stone according to state law, and if you are used to being protected as a buyer, get ready to leave that shield behind.

The seller (either the court or the trustee on behalf of the lender) does not schedule home-showing appointments like a Realtor would. You can bet that they will not allow or cooperate with you in order for you to inspect the property, will not guarantee that the title is clear (other than from first and subordinate mortgages) or that the title can be insured, will not make any warranties or disclosures including whether the property is contaminated, uninhabitable, or otherwise uninsurable, will not care if there is nefarious collusion among other bidders at the auction, will not be responsible for evicting potentially hostile occupants, and will not be responsible for recording the deed. Auctions are not for the faint of heart and are literally a *caveat emptor* (buyer beware) experience.

> *Auctions are not for the faint of heart and are literally a* caveat emptor *experience*

That doesn't mean that you are entirely helpless and at the mercy of ruthless auctioneers. It does not mean that you cannot do your own detective work: Drive by the property and inspect the outside, perform a title search, talk to neighbors, call utility and service companies, etc. But you have to take ownership and responsibility for your investment risks. You do have to put on your detective hat and realize that even your best efforts may not detect all the potential problems.

Anxious as you may be to throw your hat in the ring and begin investing, it is sage advice that you attend several auctions with your hands in your pockets before you ever start bidding. Be patient, get the experience and a feel for how auctions operate as well as the approach of other bidders.

The mechanics of buying a property at auction also function differently than they do in other types of property purchase.

Auctions generally require bidders to bring a cashier's check for a minimum amount (you will be asked to show this before you are allowed to bid) and then buyers must be able to produce the balance of the sale amount in a very short window of time—often only 24 hours. A buyer's ability to close timely is typically verified with some form of Proof of Funds (POF) requirement. Winning bidders then receive the physical deed to the property, which they must then have recorded with the county recorder's office or the register of deeds.

Auction prices start with an *opening bid*, which is typically set by the lender as a function of the balances owed on the property plus interest, bank fees, and possibly attorney's fees associated with the legal aspects of foreclosure.

If the borrower had a significant amount of equity in the property, banks may part with it for a low price. Often, however, auctions come and go with no bids that are equal or greater than the opening bid. In this case, the auction has failed to produce a buyer for the property, or failed to produce a buyer at the asking price.

If you are successful purchasing a property at auction, you should immediately have the deed recorded in your name and purchase insurance. Also, immediately inspect the property yourself and then order whatever inspections are necessary. If this property holds hidden risks that can affect the outcome of your investment, the time to discover them is sooner, rather than later.

Then you are ready to take your next steps and evaluate how you are going to go about rehabilitating and exiting the property.

Before you spend any additional cash on the property, you need make sure to protect yourself from two exceptions that haunt properties sold at a public foreclosure auction. The exceptions that investors need to be aware of are *redemption periods* and legal actions.

Typically, judicial foreclosures have a redemption period. The redemption period is a set time where the previous owner can pay off the balances owed to the bank and redeem the property—even *after* it has been sold at a public foreclosure auction.

If investors are too hasty and immediately begin making repairs on a property that they purchased at auction in anticipation of dressing the property up for sale, the possibility exists that the previous owner could still redeem the property during the redemption period with no obligation to reimburse investors for improvements they have made. (A good place to find the details of the redemption period is in the NOD.)

Protect yourself by determining whether or not your property is subject to a redemption period. If you find that it is, a tactic for mitigating the risk of a previous owner exercising his or her right of redemption is to buy the redemption rights, or better yet, get the owner to assign them to you.

The pros here are that you take control of an unknown risk in both losing the property and the time it would take waiting out the redemption period. Cons are that you may have another cost to deal with and you have to be able to negotiate for the rights with the person who holds them. Make sure that any assignment or purchase of redemption rights is done in writing with the assistance of your real estate attorney and is enforceable.

The second and related complication can be any legal action taken by the previous owner relating to the foreclosure process. Since both judicial and non-judicial foreclosures operate under the laws of the state in which they are located, there are numerous grounds upon which a *foreclosure appeal* may be based. If the legally required steps were not followed in strict accordance with the law, previous owners may sue to have the foreclosure reversed or the process reset or a number of other outcomes which are equally disruptive to your plans as an investor.

While this book should in no way be considered to offer legal advice, it is not outside the realm of possibility that as the purchaser at auction of a property with pending legal action, you may find yourself restricted from disposing of the property.

In other words, you could be prevented from making your desired exit, selling the property and realizing your profits, at the same time as you are responsible, as the owner, for carrying costs along the way. While you are holding the property but unable to sell it, you must pay for taxes, insurance, any maintenance costs that prevent further deterioration of the property, and especially worrisome in our market, you are subject to any changes in the condition of the market.

If the property is located in an area with a strong seasonal impact on real estate purchases (for instance resort communities), you could miss a critical window of opportunity. In some markets where I operate, our team has seen property values drop several percentage points *per month*. Every dollar that the property costs you is one less dollar you gain as a return when you sell.

> *Failure to sell at auction is where REOs are born*

As I mentioned, many properties do not sell at auction. The opening bid is often higher than the current market value of the property, which brings us to the next chapter: REOs. Failure to sell at auction is where REOs are born because after an auction, if there are no buyers, the property reverts to bank ownership.

CHAPTER NINE

REOs

I need to start this section with a disclosure. When it comes to my own opinions and recommendations regarding pre-foreclosure sales versus REOs, although this discussion covers all types of distressed property investing, I am personally focused primarily on investing in REOs, and not pre-foreclosure sales in the current economy.

Why? Because the market has changed.

Typically pre-foreclosure sales are great when the borrower has excess equity but for some reason cannot make the payments. This creates an opportunity to swoop in and buy out the borrower's position for less than the property is worth.

This would not have been a bad strategy in the decade leading up to the collapse of the housing bubble. Back then, it was far more common to see homeowners in this situation. However, these days, it is more common to see borrowers with negative equity who are upside-down on their first mortgage, not to mention their second. (This is the reason short selling has become more popular among pre-foreclosure investors.)

Where five years ago it might have made sense for banks to take a hard line with potential buyers and try to cover their loans plus expenses, that is not the case in today's climate where foreclosures are epidemic.

I average 40 percent cost to value in my current portfolio of REO purchases. That means I am getting a 60 percent discount to *depressed and deflated market value* on homes that have gone as far through the foreclosure process as they can go.

In my opinion, the current housing market offers a much greater opportunity for investors to buy properties at steep discounts to their market value in the REO stage, rather than at auction or in pre-foreclosure.

Buying REOs is usually done by bidding on REO properties offered by the bank. These can be offered one at a time, or in bulk. The process is more tightly guarded than other types of distressed property investing. However, throughout this book, I will be pulling back the curtain and discussing the process in detail and giving you the information you need to start investing at this level.

CHAPTER TEN

Building Your Investment Advisory Team

New investors, entrepreneurs, and business owners sometimes chafe at the cost of teaming up with other professionals. It is almost a point of pride among entrepreneurs that they have been able to build their business without help from anyone else.

However, almost all *successful* investors and entrepreneurs quickly develop relationships with professionals that they can engage to fill in critical gaps in their own understanding, expertise, and professional or trade capabilities. Distressed property investing is no different. The more you approach your foray into distressed property investing as a business venture, the better off you will be. You wouldn't start a business without an accountant or attorney, would you?

These specialists become an advisory team that ends up ensuring that you don't make foolish mistakes that turn into losses. So, who are these critical advisory team members? What are their roles and where can you find them?

The list may include (see the checklist on the following page) a real estate broker or sales agent experienced in the area in which you are making your purchase, mortgage and title professionals, a CPA with real estate experience, a financial advisor, an insurance broker, contractors and subcontractors, inspectors, appraisers and finally, a skilled real estate attorney.

With this team, *you* must provide the leadership role. You are the CEO and these are your senior executive team. They advise and counsel you, but you are in the driver's seat: You make the decisions and you live with the consequences.

Years ago I was in a discussion with my attorney. We were reviewing contracts for a fairly complex transaction, making decisions about what terms to accept and what terms to counter. My attorney was experienced and, defending my interests, explained all the ways I could get burned in the deal. A little short-sighted, I asked, "How can we make this thing work?"

To which he replied, "Well, you realize you can't let your attorney write the deal—he'll kill it every time."

I had lost sight of the fact that *I* was the decision-maker and he was just acting in his role by informing me about

Potential Members of Your Investment Advisory Team

☐ Realtor (Real Estate Broker, or Real Estate Sales Agent)
☐ Mortgage Broker
☐ Title Officer
☐ Accountant/CPA
☐ Financial Advisor
☐ Insurance broker
☐ Contractor, Subcontractor, Handyman
☐ Inspector
☐ Appraiser
☐ Real Estate Attorney

the risks. In the end, it was up to me to decide which risks were acceptable and which were not.

If you find yourself working with an advisor that tries to usurp your position as the decision-maker, you need to either realign your relationship or fire them and look for someone who understands how this type of team functions.

Also, if you *are* a professional in any of these capacities, you can decide whether or not to act in that role yourself. Note that this is still a *decision* and that I do not recommend that you automatically take on this work yourself.

For instance, if you are a real estate broker and you are familiar with the market in which you want to operate, you may want to act as your own Realtor in the deal. If, however, you are in unfamiliar territory and don't know the intricacies of the market, you may find that the wisest move is still to team up with someone who has local experience.

Let's take each advisor on the checklist in turn.

Realtor

Please note that I use the terms Realtor, real estate broker, and real estate agent more or less interchangeably because the right advisor who provides the necessary real estate buying and selling expertise could wear any of these titles. Typically, the difference between brokers and agents is a different type of state license. An agent must associate with a broker in order to represent buyers and sellers. A broker is responsible for the agents who work downstream and a broker's license allows the broker to act independently of another broker.

Think of the broker as the manager and the agents as the team. Then realize that there are exceptions. Some agents are more skilled than some brokers, but are content to work under a broker for their entire career.

Both brokers and agents can be Realtors, which means members of the National Association of Realtors (NAR). The NAR is a trade association, which provides resources, training, and lobbying on behalf of real estate professionals. However, membership is voluntary and not required by the law (but over half of all real estate professionals are members of the NAR.)

Now, what are the considerations you should have when deciding whether or not to add a Realtor to your team?

Realtors don't work for free. You will have to plan on paying them a commission for transactions they work on. You will need to account for this expense as you evaluate your ability to turn a profit on each deal.

What they offer in return could be local expertise, networking connections with the potential to help you make a quick sale, find a great property, or connect with other team members like mortgage brokers or contractors. They may have access to a Multiple Listing Service (MLS) or several MLS databases, which is an invaluable source of information when both buying and selling. They might have the experience of many transactions and critical advice for you in the process of buying and selling a property—what price is too high or too low, marketing and advertising tools they have found effective, staging and selling tips. What's more, this advice may be specialized in a type of property or a specific market that you want to invest in.

What do you want to look for in a Realtor? In addition to being able to develop a good working relationship, here are some things to consider: Advanced certifications (like Graduate Realtor Institute or GRI, Certified Residential Specialist or CRS, etc.), comparative performance in the marketplace, length of experience (some Realtors burn out quickly), technical savvy (do they have a web site, blog, and evidence of competent use of the Internet in their business), support staff, recommendations from customers and colleagues, and community involvement.

You may also evaluate them based on their personality. Are they proactive, happy to do the legwork to close deals, and available and accessible to you? Will they be afraid to submit low offers? Have they been involved in distressed property investing before with others or even as investors themselves? Will they work comfortably with you as an advisor?

Mortgage Brokers and Title Officers

Mortgage brokers can help you secure financing for your subject properties and provide a valuable service that you may be able to offer to your potential buyers. Neither the buying nor the selling will happen without the right financing.

Establishing connections with a title company can help you facilitate title searches, keep closings running smoothly, and offer valuable connections to others working in your area. Your ability to detect liens, clouds, and encumbrances will directly impact your ability to exit and profit from an investment property. I always try to have someone on my team who can advise me on the implications of anything affecting my ability to get title insurance.

CPA and Financial Advisor

These don't have to be the same person, but they can be. With transactions as large as they typically are in real estate investing, you want someone in your corner who can advise you on the tax implications of a deal. You need to know how to receive and categorize the proceeds of your investments.

Likewise, a skilled financial advisor may be able to help you keep more of the money you earn and form a plan that will help you safeguard your long-term financial health.

Insurance Broker

As you complete more and more real estate deals, you will want a go-to advisor for insurance. You are going to need insurance on the property from the moment you take ownership, and you may need specialized insurance help if, for instance, your investment property is located in a flood plain and requires flood insurance.

Contractors, Subcontractors, Handymen

I include a more detailed discussion of hiring contractors in Chapter 29, "Finding a Contractor," but here I want to emphasize the value of building relationships with professionals you can trust. Having contractors on your speed dial who you know are skilled in their execution of the work, trustworthy and accurate in their estimates, and honest and fair in their billing is very valuable. Interviewing contractors and reviewing bids takes a lot of time. Having someone you can trust is a critical component to keeping your costs under control and your timeline as short as possible.

I list contractors, subcontractors and handymen and here's why. For big jobs, you need a general contractor who oversees the work of multiple subcontractors (professionals who are licensed to perform contract work of a specific type like plumbing or electrical work). Some jobs are less extensive and you can manage subcontractors directly, effectively doing the job of a contractor yourself. And then there are jobs which are appropriate for the skills of a handyman, and for which hiring a contractor would create a disproportionate expense.

In any category, you want to look for dirt and callouses. You want to find someone who isn't afraid of hard work.

Inspectors and Appraisers

Specifics on inspections are discussed in the Due Diligence section on page 85, but having a third party for validating your estimation of an investment property's value and for double-checking your repair and rehabilitation estimates can be extremely valuable. Often you can find inspectors who used to be local building inspectors or who have worked in a capacity that they are intimately familiar with building codes and construction professionals in the local area.

Real Estate Attorney

Of all the members of my investment advisory team, the most critical member, the one I would *never* be without, is my real estate attorney. Under certain circumstances, I might choose to forego the services of any of the other members, but not this one.

The best advice I have on choosing a good attorney is that, with a good one, you will feel like you maybe aren't paying enough. The value created and the level of service are so high, that you wonder why you aren't being charged more. The reverse is also true, no matter how cheap a bad attorney is, you always feel like you are paying too much because the value and service is so poor.

A good attorney will have specialized experience in real estate transactions, will be familiar with the particulars of contract law in your area and will be constantly protecting your interests. They will be your go-to resource when submitting and reviewing contracts and for negotiations with other attorneys who may represent buyers or sellers in a transaction or represent the lenders and banks who are negotiating the sale of their REOs.

With a solid team in place, it's time to start finding those deals.

CHAPTER ELEVEN

Preparing a Profile

What is the first step? Where do you start? How do you go about finding an imminent foreclosure, or an REO property?

Being well-prepared is one of the keys to making your foray into distressed property investing a success. I recommend that before you start looking for properties, you establish some criteria—a *profile* for the type of property you are interested in. This profile is a set of criteria that you will use to build a dossier on potential investment properties. It will guide you so you don't spend all your time looking for the wrong type of property or looking in the wrong place.

Depending on where you are looking, you may find that there are way too many properties to sort through. Your profile also acts like a filter to weed out those properties that don't meet your primary investment criteria. Why waste time on deals that aren't really what you are looking for?

When you are building your profile, ask yourself questions like: What is my price range? What can I really afford to put in to this investment? REO deals can range from tens or hundreds of thousands of dollars to tens or hundreds of millions and more. That's a broad range and if you don't know which area of the market you are interested in and at what level you are capable of playing, your chances of a costly misstep are much greater.

> **"You need a line in the sand that keeps your investment intact"**

You may also want to ask yourself: What locations am I willing to look at? What is my exit strategy? What type of property fits my goals and expectations? For example, are you primarily interested in some flavor of residential property like single-family residences, multifamily condos or apartments, or do you prefer commercial property, industrial property, or raw land? Where is your expertise and interest?

Your background may have equipped you to be familiar with the type of repairs and refurbishment that is common for office space, but not the issues involved with an apartment building or single-family home.

Ask yourself how much rehab work am I equipped to perform? Do I need properties that require little, if any, additional work, or can I tackle major construction projects? How much can I afford in repair and refurbishment?

Finally, no profile would be complete without an anticipated margin. You need a line in the sand that keeps your investment intact. If the terms of a deal fall outside the parameters you have set out for yourself, it is time to walk away.

Believe me, this is much easier to do if you have made your decision criteria clear right from the beginning.

Try to use criteria in your profile that helps you easily compare properties that you encounter. To be an effective decision-making tool, your profile should capture the critical metrics in your decision-making. Are you looking for absolutely the biggest margin potential, or are you better served by properties that require little or no rehab and that you can turn quickly? There is no profile that works for every investor. Your job is to craft one that is tailored to your individual and specific needs.

The preparation and organization required to build a well thought out investment property profile will give you measurable indicators that you can use to navigate through an otherwise emotional process. By outlining the characteristics of your target property, you can begin looking for properties without fear of being overwhelmed by all the possibilities or the hidden factors you may discover once you get out there.

CHAPTER TWELVE

Financing

Understanding the characteristics of your ideal property has to be cast against the backdrop of your financial options. Your possibilities should limit your criteria before your preferences.

In other words, your ability to finance the purchase must be in place *before* you go looking for distressed property. The reason for this is that the best opportunities are very time-sensitive. If you cannot come with the cash, the deal will go to someone else.

Now, having cash doesn't necessarily mean you have these amounts sitting around. You can acquire the necessary cash via financing, but you have to have the ability to drop a certified check for the purchase amount and you have to have it immediately available. In finance terms, cash represents liquidity. In order to take advantage of the greatest number of opportunities investing in distressed property, you must have sufficient liquidity to execute.

I like the following list[11] from Ralph R. Roberts describing the benefits of cash:

Credibility: Cash gives you the ability to execute on your promise to purchase. It's the "money talks" idiom and when you have the cash, people listen.

Confidence: With cash in your pocket, you can strike deals knowing you can back up your offers.

Creativity: Cash allows you to be creative in how you structure a deal because you are not limited by your financial approach. It gives you ultimate flexibility.

Competitiveness: Being able to execute a deal ahead of competitors gives you an edge and increases the chance that homeowners and banks will listen to what you have to say.

There is a checklist on the following page, which is designed to help ensure that you are financially prepared to execute when the right deal presents itself.

> **If you cannot come with the cash, the deal will go to someone else**

In order to ensure that you can get the financing you need, make sure that your individual credit is in good shape. Don't let a few dollars in missed payments or mistakes cost you thousands. Frequently check your credit score and contest errors.

You may also have access to funds by borrowing against your own home, dipping into savings or retirement accounts, borrowing money from family or friends, and pursuing the hard money lenders. Each of these approaches has merits and drawbacks, but distressed property investing

Financing Options Checklist

Cash

☐ How much cash do I have on hand?

☐ Do I need to liquidate an asset in order to secure the necessary cash?

☐ Does my access to cash limit my time frame?

Cash and Debt

☐ Is my debt financing lined up?

☐ Am I prequalified for the necessary amount?

☐ How long do I expect my lender will take to fund?

Partnership

☐ Will I partner with others to do this deal?

☐ Are the terms of our arrangement clear and agreed upon by all parties?

☐ Do I anticipate delays from my partner(s)?

is not a risk-free operation and judging which risks are right for you and which are not is part of the experience you must gain in order to be successful. With your profile and financing in order, you are ready to go hunting for deals.

Finding

CHAPTER THIRTEEN

Which Rocks to Look Under: Public Records

For individual investors, a good place to start looking for information about these properties is with public records and local publications. Anyone investing in real estate should become familiar with these resources.

Public property records are typically filed with the county clerk at the county recorder's office.[12] These are handled at the county level, just like property taxes. As I mentioned, certain notices are required to be recorded during the foreclosure process. You should be able to search for NODs, Notices of Sale, or *lis pendens*[13] filings.

There is usually no cost for searching public records and they are available to anyone. Notices filed with the county recorder's office are also very current. You are likely to find properties that have not yet been added to the lists compiled by listing services or online providers.

The drawback is that you are limited to only one county recorder's office at a time. Internet resources for county records vary drastically from county to county (meaning that you will likely need to plan on visiting these offices in person), and searching these resources can be very time-consuming, especially if you are unfamiliar with the process.

However, county recorder's offices (or the office of the register of deeds) are typically staffed with people who can help you get familiar with the process. Being courteous and polite can often get you a long way with the staff at these offices and they often represent a wealth of knowledge about not only how records can be searched, but about the process the filers go through to record their notices.

> *Anyone investing in real estate should become familiar with public records*

Notices of Sale typically must also be published in the local newspaper (depending on the local regulations, these notices may be required to be published more than once during the period leading up to the sale). By searching local business journals and newspapers under their Public Notice sections, you can find sale notices. In order to save yourself some wasted time, you may want to look up which newspapers are required for the posting of legal notices. Sometimes these are small local papers, and sometimes they are a dominant paper in the area.

CHAPTER FOURTEEN

More Finding Opportunities

The types of notices described in the preceding section typically apply to properties that are in the pre-foreclosure stage on their way to a public foreclosure auction. What about bank-owned properties? There are no notices required for properties that failed to sell at auction. However, just like pre-foreclosures, when a property becomes an REO, your finding opportunity starts with identifying who owns it.

The owner is typically going to be the lender—a bank or other financial institution—although various government entities also have the power to foreclose or seize properties (these entities range from the IRS and Fannie Mae to seizures made by U.S. Customs or the U.S. Marshals Service).[14] You can also check with local government offices (typically at the county level) to see if they have a list of tax foreclosures. All of these potential holders of foreclosed property have processes they go through when foreclosing or trying to sell the foreclosed properties.

There are a few methods for identifying properties that are in the REO pools of banks and lenders.

The Internet can be a great resource in your search for REO properties. Many real estate brokerages compile lists of foreclosures in the areas they serve. In addition, several significant financial institutions list their REO properties on their company web sites (Countrywide, now owned by Bank of America, Washington Mutual, now owned by Chase, and secondary mortgage market players like Fannie Mae to name a few—a more lengthy list is provided in the Appendix).

Most have tools for sorting through properties to refine your search (although the search criteria may be limited). You may be able to sort by city, price, number of bedrooms, and other criteria.

There are also listing service companies who provide lists of REO properties for a fee. (A list of some of these is provided in the Appendix.) There are literally hundreds of these online.[15,16] Many, like RealtyTrac.com or Foreclosure.com offer a free trial and then charge a periodic fee. Some, like REO Source offer their more limited services for free.

Listing services can cover regional or national scope and, compared with lender web sites, offer more information about properties in various stages of foreclosure, including the notices filed with the county as well as additional information regarding the loans on the property and sometimes even contact information.

A word of caution about online resources: If you decide to use one of these, be wary of scams and deceptive marketing practices. I have tried to include only reputable resources, but make sure you do your homework before paying anyone. Make sure you look for third-party validation that the company is legitimate. Ask around on Internet forums or consumer protection sites before giving anyone your money or credit card information.

Sometimes you can find REO properties by going through an asset management company. These companies are like listing agents for lenders with a focus on the disposition of REO properties. They tend to buy or represent bulk *REO tapes*.

Typical REO tapes contain between 20 and 500 homes (although they can contain more). Bulk tapes are available at a discount that is typically unavailable to individual investors buying a single property.

Just like banks these companies are motivated to sell and sometimes will perform some of the tests or rehab work required on the property in advance in order to make the sale look more attractive.[17] One of the benefits of dealing with an asset management company is that these companies have had a chance to build relationships with banks which could be impossible, or at least very time consuming for individual investors to cultivate. Some of them will specialize in buying REO tapes and then selling the properties off individually. Many asset management companies provide REO property listings on their websites.[18] (A list of asset management companies can be found in the Appendix.)

This brings me to one of the truly indispensable parts of serious REO investing and that is relationships with the lenders. This is probably the toughest hurdle for new investors looking to break into REO investing because the relationships are built up over years and cemented by consistent transaction performance.

In my own company, the relationships we have with banks and asset managers allows us to access some of the best tapes early in the process and search for the prime opportunities ahead of many other investors.

Even if you are just getting started (and everyone has to start somewhere), begin forming these relationships. Leverage relationships within your investment advisory team. If you have a Realtor that has relationships with key bank personnel, use that connection to get introduced. Learn to contact department managers in a way that is helpful to them. Add value for anyone you connect with through your professional network.

Managers at bank loan loss mitigation departments or home loan trading departments are already overwhelmed and the last thing they need is a string of phone calls and letters from the latest crop of attendees at a local seminar on foreclosures. They neither want nor do they have the time to educate amateur investors, few of whom will ever develop the capacity to help the bank dispose of properties in its REO pool.

Unlikely as it may seem, another potential finding opportunity is within homeowner's associations. HOAs often know about financial distress early because homeowners in trouble stop paying their association dues. By the same token, HOAs are interested in getting people out who don't pay and people in who do, so they may be inclined to talk with you. These communities are like villages and often the HOA officers are the busybodies that will have all the gossip within their community. It may surprise you what you can learn from these people. If the area in which you are targeting for investment has some communities, it may take very little time to reach out and discover distressed properties.

Be cautious as you establish new relationships in the distressed property investing community. For every legitimate company working in this trade, there are dozens of companies that are attracted by the big dollars, but who do not have the capacity to really get a deal done. I recommend that you waste as little time as possible dealing with people who claim to represent others. Legitimate sellers actually *want* to find legitimate buyers, so I recommend that you be wary of deals that sound too good to be true, parties that are reclusive, and middlemen that get in the way and screw up the deal.

Another resource for finding REO deals, as well as resources you can trust to help you gain experience investing, is local clubs or organizations. Many areas have privately organized real estate investing clubs. Joining a club like this could be an opportunity to network with others who have been down the distressed property investing road before and who may have valuable insights about dealing with local conditions, and opportunities that exist within your local market.

Now let's say you have established your profile, you have got your financing lined up, and you have successfully found a number of properties that fit your criteria. What next?

> *Before you start making bids or submitting offers, you have some homework to do*

Before you start making bids or submitting offers, you have some homework to do. It may be helpful to think of the process of investing in distressed real estate as a business venture rather than simply an investment in the traditional sense. Just like managing a company, you will need to manage these steps and the processes and people within them to maximize your chances of a return. This leads us to the next step, which is *due diligence*.

Due Diligence

CHAPTER FIFTEEN

Uncovering a House's Secrets

A home inspector once told me, "Every home has its secrets." This is something my own experience has taught me to be true many times over.

Not everyone performs a physical on-site inspection before purchasing a distressed property. That does not mean you should skip this step. In fact, in order to protect yourself, you need to become an expert at inspecting properties.

When you do an on-site inspection of a potential investment property, you aren't a casual home buyer, you are Sherlock Holmes. You need look past the surface. It helps to have an attitude like you would expect from a detective on *CSI*, that if there are any problems here, come hell or high water, you are going to find them. Remember who is on the line if the deal goes bad. The person writing the

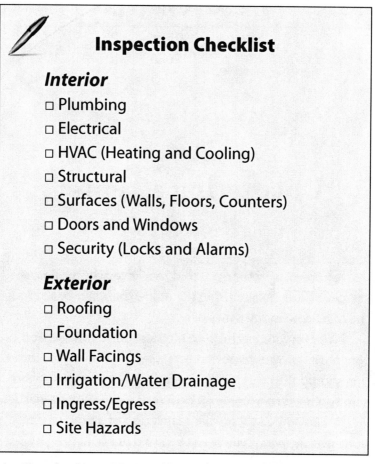

Inspection Checklist

Interior
- ☐ Plumbing
- ☐ Electrical
- ☐ HVAC (Heating and Cooling)
- ☐ Structural
- ☐ Surfaces (Walls, Floors, Counters)
- ☐ Doors and Windows
- ☐ Security (Locks and Alarms)

Exterior
- ☐ Roofing
- ☐ Foundation
- ☐ Wall Facings
- ☐ Irrigation/Water Drainage
- ☐ Ingress/Egress
- ☐ Site Hazards

check is the one who is ultimately responsible for *every-thing*—and that's you.

And just like those crime-scene technicians that carry around a tote full of specialized tools, you need to be prepared with a few items yourself.

For instance, you probably want to bring a flashlight, digital camera, measuring tape, basic toolkit (pliers, screwdrivers, etc.), a checklist, and a way to take notes (clipboard, notebook, voice recorder, etc.) on what you find. You may find electronic tools useful like a laptop computer or Internet enabled smart phone or PDA so you can search for additional information you may not have realized was important until you arrived on location. Remember to keep spare memory cards, batteries, and any other supplies that might be required.

I recommend that when you approach a new property you work from the outside in—after all, that is how your potential buyers will experience the property. Train your eye to see untapped potential, starting with curb appeal. Learn to discern between cosmetic problems like ghastly colors, superficial damage, or neglected landscaping, which are relatively inexpensive to correct, and serious structural, systemic, or neighborhood problems that are expensive or impossible to repair.

Learn how to evaluate a building's systems. Check the utilities, if possible. Learn how to inspect the power, natural gas, and other heating systems. Know whether the building is connected to public sewer or has a septic tank.

Water damage is one of the most common and expensive problems in any type of building. Learn to detect signs of poor drainage, leaks, and previous plumbing problems. Call utility companies and ask for a record of complaints, on-site calls, and repairs.

Training yourself to detect problems is a skill that goes against the emotional flow of buying a home you want to live in. Rather than picturing your hopes and dreams in the castle you hope to put around your family, you are hunting for things that will undermine your investment. If you want to practice (and this is a skill worth practicing as much as you can for free—before you have your own money on the line), try to attend some open houses for properties at the lower end of the price spectrum. Don't rely on what the Realtor tells you, just tour the property and scrutinize it as much as you can and see what you are able to detect. Make a critical inspection checklist and then see what you can add to it as you visit the next home.

Some types of disasters require special cleanup. You need to know if the property has had a flood, fire, mold problem, has been a meth house, or is otherwise contaminated. These flaws could affect your ability to get insurance, whether the home is uninhabitable, and eventually your ability to sell the property.

This kind of basic due diligence is generally possible at little or no cost. However, its value is tremendous when weighed against the cost of missing something that should have tipped you off that you were buying a money pit.

CHAPTER SIXTEEN

Professional Inspector?

There is an industry of professional building inspectors with various specialties. This means that there are several types of inspections that you can pay to have performed. As a general rule it is cheaper to pay for an inspection before you own the property than it is to fix a problem that went undetected during due diligence.

You need to weigh the cost of an inspection with your stage of evaluation. You may want to reserve professional inspections as a condition of your purchase contract or use their findings as a point of negotiation (more on this in the Contract and Close section).

Typically, for a few hundred dollars you can hire a professional inspector to perform a whole-house inspection. A sample home inspection checklist is included in the Appendix. Often these inspectors will provide a guarantee or even some type of limited warranty for those items included in their inspection. (Remember, unlike homes on the

91

regular real estate market, REO properties will generally be sold *as-is* with no warranty at all. When you buy it, you are 100 percent responsible for anything that is wrong or goes wrong with the property, so having a guarantee from an inspector could be valuable.) Inspectors may also have specialized equipment to test for water damage, gas leaks, and harmful radon gas.

Look for someone who is a member of the National Institute of Building Inspectors (NIBI).[19] Watch them closely in order to learn things that might help you in performing your own inspections.

You will very likely need a pest inspection. You may need to factor in costs for termite treatments, repair of structural damage or exterminators for rodents or insects.

Houses built before 1978 may contain lead-based paint. This becomes poisonous to people and especially dangerous to children when the paint flakes off or crumbles to dust. Inspectors can test for lead-based paint. Even though buying a home this way will probably mean that you don't see a disclosure about lead-based paint, you will need to provide one when you sell.

Finally, if either your own inspection or the one you pay to have performed expose significant problems with the property—problems that erode your margin to an unacceptable level or which introduce sufficient unknown costs into your investment equation—be willing to walk away. The few hundred dollars that you may lose on an inspection is not worth losing thousands on an investment that could unravel on you. In order to help assess costs that you may underestimate, or which may creep in scope, I recommend that you err on the side of caution and assume hidden costs will expand and then ask yourself if it is still worth it to pursue this property.

CHAPTER SEVENTEEN

Rehab Estimates

One of the most critical factors that will determine whether you make money or lose it will be your ability to accurately estimate the cost and value of expected repairs to the property.

Repair costs have a way of spiraling out of control and taking longer to complete than estimated. Both end up eating away at the return you hope to make on your investment. More than a few house flippers end up scrambling to get out with their skin on. You will need to quickly become a master estimator and skilled manager of the subcontractors you hire to do this work.

During your inspections you will compile a list of required repairs—those things that you think will bring a greater return than their cost and which will, in the aggregate, increase your chance of exiting your investment quickly or on the most favorable terms. As you build that list of repairs, you will find that some repairs are deal breakers.

What I mean is that some repairs can be so extensive that the risk is inordinately high that they will destroy your margin. These are especially critical when they affect the safety and structural integrity of the home.

Examples of this type of problem are: Cracks in the foundation, decay in bearing walls or structural members, contamination, water issues (especially those likely to recur), etc. When I see this type of problem, I generally walk away and recommend you do the same.

Another acceptable option, however, is to negotiate a concession in price that truly reflects the risk associated with the problem. Sometimes that means you are negotiating at the value of only the land because it is cheaper to tear the house down than to fix it.

It is also important to determine which repairs are important and which are not. Our company often sells its properties *as-is* because we think the return on investment for certain types of refurbishment are not worth the time and effort. On the other hand, sometimes relatively inexpensive repairs like paint and carpeting can dramatically improve how a property shows to potential buyers. When you estimate repair costs, make sure you expect to reap a margin on those costs equal to the percentage margin you expected from the property to begin with.

CHAPTER EIGHTEEN

Occupancy

Just because a home has been foreclosed on, does not mean the occupants are gone. Eviction laws vary state by state, but it is not uncommon for eviction to be a lengthy and difficult process. Eviction time frames range from 30 days to over a year. Occupants (former owners or renters) are frequently informed about avoiding eviction and how to stay in the home as long as possible.

You need to be aware of any occupants and the risks they represent. As long as they occupy the property, they may continue to deteriorate the value of the property through abuse or lack of proper maintenance. They may also be uncooperative with your due diligence efforts. If you anticipate needing to evict the occupants, allow for the legal costs and the extended time frame in your budget.

In my experience around 30 percent of REO properties have still had occupants by the time we purchased the properties. To deal with occupants, in our company, we frequently take a *cash for keys* approach to limit our exposure. Cash for Keys means that we essentially offer the occupants a bribe to vacate the property.

If the property was a judicial foreclosure and the previous owners have redemption rights, you should condition the cash for keys offer on either an assignment of redemption rights or a nonredemption certificate. Have your attorney draft it, and get it signed by the party who legally holds the redemption rights before you cough up any cash.

In principle, if these occupants were flush with cash, they could probably pay for lodging like everybody else. That means that they are often strapped for cash and relatively small amounts can be enough to entice them to vacate. It is often cheaper to pay them to leave than it is to execute all the legal proceedings to have them evicted by court order and removed.

Other soft incentives may include paying for a moving truck, paying the deposit on the new rental home the family is moving to, or even something as simple as providing a dumpster for them to get rid of articles that they don't want to take with them.

CHAPTER NINETEEN

Appraisal/Valuation

So far our discussion of due diligence has focused on uncovering hidden costs associated with the property. It is simply the most cost-effective approach to be thorough and avoid getting surprised by something you should have caught during the early due diligence phase.

Once you account for any potential losses due to hidden repairs or refurbishment, you need to estimate your top-side. As part of your due diligence, you need to establish what the property's value will be when you expect to sell it. This is often referred to as your After Repair Value (ARV) and reflects the realistic amount of cash you expect to walk away with when you sell. A mistake here can be just as detrimental to your investment as being blind-sided by hidden costs.

Your ARV needs to be grounded in reality. For Example, don't fool yourself into thinking that your repairs will produce a $500,000 house in a $200,000 neighborhood.

What you want is a realistic understanding of the homes value in the market where it sits.

Start by looking for *comparables*—homes that meet similar criteria to your desired property that have recently sold. The more alike they are, the better in terms of square footage, age, number of bedrooms and bathrooms, amenities, lot size, location and condition.

Comparables will give you a relative ballpark estimate of the selling price you should be able to get. The idea is that the performance of similar properties in the same general location ought to be fairly accurate predictors of how your property will perform.

> *You want to be neither optimistic nor pessimistic here, but realistic*

Both high- and low-selling comparables are useful. You will want information on low-selling comparable to present to the bank when you submit your bid. The mixture of other comparables will help you get a fair sense of the price the market ought to bring. You want to be neither optimistic nor pessimistic here, but realistic.

Don't forget to consider how much price you might need to give up to meet your target sales time frame. In other words, you should expect to sell your property for less if you expect to find a buyer in 30 days, than you would if you expect to find a buyer in 90 days.

There are several resources you can access to get information on comparables. You can get a general indication for residential property values from web sites like Cyberhomes.com, PropertyShark.com, and Zillow.com. These sites use a variety of comparable data as well as public records to establish a generic valuation. While they are useful for indicating a ballpark figure, they can run high or low depending on the quality of the underlying data. You should use them as a general indicator only and not rely on their estimates alone.

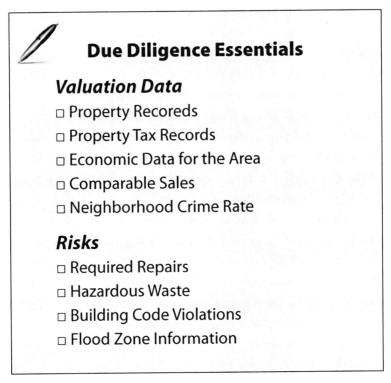

Due Diligence Essentials

Valuation Data
☐ Property Recoreds
☐ Property Tax Records
☐ Ecomonic Data for the Area
☐ Comparable Sales
☐ Neighborhood Crime Rate

Risks
☐ Required Repairs
☐ Hazardous Waste
☐ Building Code Violations
☐ Flood Zone Information

If you plan on using a Realtor as part of your investment advisory team, they will likely have access to a Multiple Listing Service (MLS). An MLS is a computer database of properties listed for sale by Realtors who subscribe to it. Historical data within the MLS will tell you about the sales history of other properties in the neighborhood—what they listed for, what they sold for, and how many days they spent on the market before selling.

Also consider factors present in the market in general. Look at the job market and the business climate. People move where they can find work and changes in the job market will affect your ability to sell the property. For instance, has a large employer in the neighborhood recently gone through layoffs leaving many homes on the market and few new buyers? Has an announcement of a new project or plant brought new people into the area? Is local unemployment up or down compared to the region? How much do the *trades* impact the job market—in other words those jobs related to housing itself—jobs like construction trades, real estate and mortgage brokers.

Take a good look at the neighborhood, the schools, key employers nearby, and access to shopping and healthcare facilities. Look at who is living in the neighborhood. Are they mostly students or retirees? Are they young families or empty nesters? The type of buyer the market has attracted in the past is a pretty good indicator about who will be interested in the future. See if you can establish a target buyer for your type of property and consider what benefits you will offer to that buyer even at this early stage.

In our company, we saw a property that had originally been listed for $1.8 million. It had been on the market for some time with no buyers. The price dropped to $1.5 million, then $1.3 million. It dropped to $900 thousand before entering foreclosure. It was eventually offered to us at $400 thousand.

You would think that we would have jumped all over this deal. How often do you see a property that has been reduced by $1.4 million!

In our due diligence process, however, we identified that the neighborhood was occupied primarily by Realtors, contractors, and mortgage brokers. The neighbors' driveways were full of expensive cars and ski boats. This told us that the other owners were all players in the housing business and were heavily leveraged.

We expected most of the neighborhood to go into foreclosure eventually, and decided that our maximum bid was about $250 thousand. This offer was not accepted, and the bank even indicated that they had accepted another offer. But, when the next round of REO tapes from this lender came around, we noticed the property was simply relisted and at the time of this writing still has not sold.

Look for indicators that the market is hot or cold—commonly described as either a buyer's market or a seller's market.

A seller's market means that buyers are plentiful and sellers can afford to take only the best deals that come along. Signs of a seller's market include: Very little inventory (i.e., relatively few homes for sale), quick sales measured in terms of Days on the Market (DOM). These conditions can result in multiple offers and even bidding wars where homes sell for more than the asking price

A buyer's market is the opposite. More homes are available than ready buyers to take them, so buyers are in a strong position to negotiate for what they want. You will notice that in this type of market, homes are listed and spending many more DOM, generally over 120 days, without offers.

Seller's trying to avoid the stigma of too many days on the market will attempt to reset their DOM by re-listing the property. Some communities have enacted laws that require properties to stay off the market for a period of time, typically about 90 days, before they can re-list and reset their DOM clock.

Analysts describe the inventory in terms of how many months it will take at the current rate of sales to absorb the inventory on the market. The current market has some areas of the country carrying a 24-month inventory or more, and that does not include new homes being listed for sale.

Although not a guarantee, this information can help you determine what price you can get for your property. It can also help you estimate what you need to accept if you want a fast sale.

With a clear picture of your costs, the ARV will tell you what you need to calculate the margin you expect to make on the property. It can be helpful to look at the margin on these deals in terms of percentages. For example, $50,000 in profit potential on a $550,000 home represents a much thinner margin than $50,000 in profit potential on a home worth $150,000.

In our company, we specifically look for deals that have enough margin for a speedy transaction. Our typical property is under contract within 13 days or less and our average number of days to close is 42.

By establishing enough margin as your target, you are flexible to adjust as conditions require. If your margins are too tight, for example, you won't be free to adjust for a quick sale and avoid the risks of a distended holding time.

Also, do not forget to figure in 6 to 9 percent of the final price toward closing costs and real estate commissions if you decide to use a Realtor.

CHAPTER TWENTY

Valuing Income Property

Rental properties are valued differently than individual houses for sale. They likewise use comparables as part of their valuation process, but the valuation analysis uses terms and techniques more common for traditional investing.

Income property is looked at as a business that produces income. As such, metrics for how the property produces income and return on investment (ROI) are customary. However, just like single-family residences, valuing rental property begins with comparables.

These valuations consider comparable rents as well as the occupancy levels and value of comparable properties. For residential properties these may be a simple calculation based on bedroom and bathroom configuration and square footage. For commercial property, it is likely a rate per square foot for a similar class of commercial property.

For example, most office space is considered Class A (in practice, this is so common that Class A has become practically meaningless as a standard for evaluating the quality of an office building). In your market it may be typical to see annual rents anywhere from $25 to $250 per square foot. In some areas of Manhattan, the rate has been over $1,000 per square foot.

Rental property valuation methods then consider the business processes that produce income. They are valued as much for the revenue stream they produce as they are for the market value the property would bring in a sale.

A quick rule of thumb is the *gross rent multiplier* (GRM). GRM is calculated by dividing the sales price by the annual rents. In this example (Figure 3) we compare two properties based on their GRM. All things being equal, the lower the GRM, the better value the property because you earn more income for the amount of money you have to spend.[20] In the example shown here, property #2 gives us a better GRM.

GRM, however, does not take into account many of the factors that impact

Figure 3: EXAMPLE: GROSS RENT MULTIPLIER (GRM)

	Prop #1	Prop #2
Units	25	40
Rent	$1,200	$900
Monthly	$30,000	$36,000
Annual Revenue	$360,000	$432,000
Sales Price	$3,500,000	$3,500,000
Price per Unit	$140,000	$87,500
GRM	9.72	8.10
(GRM = Sales Price ÷ Annual Revenue)		

the profitability of an income property and so, in practice, is not used as anything more than a simple rule of thumb.

One of the more common valuation methods is determining the *capitalization rate* or *cap rate* of the subject property.

Cap rate looks at the *net income* of the property before taxes. To calculate the cap rate, first subtract your operating expenses from your gross rents and then divide the sales price by the net (Figure 4).

Another way of thinking about Cap rate is that it is an expression of how long it will take for the investment to repay your initial capital. In other words, if you received all the money you spent to acquire the property back in the first year, your cap rate would be 100, or 100 percent. In this respect, investors familiar with the stock market could equate cap rate to a P/E ratio (price to earnings ratio)—a metric often used to compare the performance of individual stocks.

Essentially, a higher cap rate is better for buyers and a lower one is better for sellers.

Figure 4: EXAMPLE: CAPITALIZATION "CAP" RATE

	Prop #1	Prop #2
Units	25	40
Rent	$1,200	$900
Monthly	$30,000	$36,000
Annual Revenue	$360,000	$432,000
Sales Price	$3,500,000	$3,500,000
Price per Unit	$140,000	$87,500
Expenses	$150,000	$240,000
Net Income	$210,000	$192,000
Cap Rate	**0.34**	**0.41**

(Cap Rate = Sales Price ÷ Net Income)

In this example (which uses the same terms as the GRM example), property #2 has a cap rate of 18.23, meaning that it would take us five and a half years to get our initial investment back. property #1, however, would take a full six years to generate that much income. Since we are looking to buy, this makes property #2 a more attractive investment.

Knowing the sources and amounts of the expenses it takes to operate the property should be considered the bare minimum of information when evaluating an income property. In this example (for the sake of comparison), both properties spend $500 per month per unit in operating expenses.

GRM did not include any information at all about the expenses relating to the property, but the cap rate approach shows us that even though property #2 has $90,000 more in expenses each year (due to more units), the extra income offsets that risk and it continues to be the better choice of the two.

Yet another quick-check method of evaluating rental property is the *cash on cash* return method (Figure 5). Cash on cash is calculated by dividing the cash flow (annual income) of the property by how much cash is required to close the deal (in this case, the down payment). This is sometimes shown as a percentage.

The first rule of finance is *never run out of cash*. In this analysis, investors want to see how much cash outlay is required to complete the purchase in relation to how

Figure 5: EXAMPLE: CASH ON CASH

	Prop #1	Prop #2
Units	25	40
Rent	$1,200	$900
Monthly	$30,000	$36,000
Annual Revenue	$360,000	$432,000
Sales Price	$3,500,000	$3,500,000
Price per Unit	$140,000	$87,500
Down Payment	$1,050,000	$1,050,000
Cash on Cash	0.34	0.41
(Cash on Cash = Annual Revenue ÷ Cash Outlay)		

much cash flow the property generates. It is a method that takes into consideration the time-value of money (i.e., cash flow today is worth more than cash flow tomorrow) and the impact of financing on the deal when some of the purchase is made with debt.

For instance, let's say that we again compare property #1 and property #2, but this time we add that we intend to pay 30 percent of the purchase price as a down payment, and finance the remainder. 30 percent of $3.5 million is $1,050,000.

With cash on cash, the higher the number, the better. The higher cash on cash return shown for property #2 indicates that for the amount of cash required, this property generates the greatest amount of cash in return.

Cash on cash return is limited like GRM in that it does not account for expenses. Its calculation only includes gross revenues, not net income. It also does not distinguish between income and *return of capital* (ROC). Nor does it take into account appreciation, depreciation or compounding interest which all have the potential to change the financial model and desirability of a deal.

These analyses all show us results over a single period; in our example, that period is one year. However, these investments are typically multi-year with terms adjusting each year for inflation, appreciation, etc. By estimating each of these years, we can apply some more sophisticated investment tools to our analysis and gain an even more sophisticated understanding of the estimated valuation of an income property.

Net Present Value (NPV) analysis is at the center of this type of valuation and, like cash on cash essentially accounts for the time value of money, but does so over specific consecutive periods of time. NPV calculates the current value of positive and negative cash flows over a range of periods. For our example, we are using a six-year range with revenues and expenses summed for each year. The formula for calculating NPV looks like Figure 6:

However, if you have not worked your way through one of these formulas since college (and frankly, even if you have), you will find it much easier to use the tools built into

Figure 6: NET PRESENT VALUE (NPV) FORMULA

$$NPV = \sum_{t-1}^{T} \frac{C_t}{(1+r)^t} - C_o$$

Microsoft Excel or another spreadsheet program to calculate NPV on deals of this type.

Using Excel, we can calculate NPV by using the discount rate (also called our *cost of capital* or our *required rate of return*—this represents how much we might reasonably expect to get as a rate of return on an alternative investment and becomes the factor by which we measure the time value of money), and the before-tax positive and negative cash flows anticipated for each period. In this example (Figure 7), we assumed a 3 percent inflation factor in both our expenses and our ability to raise the rents. In addition to operating expenses, we included the up front expense we incurred as the down payment in year one.

Both properties show a positive NPV occurring between year six and seven. At

Figure 7: EXAMPLE: NPV

	Prop #1	Prop #2
Discount Rate	10%	10%
Year 1		
Revenue	$360,000	$432,000
Expenses	($1,200,000)	($1,290,000)
Year 2		
Revenue	$370,800	$444,960
Expenses	($154,500)	($247,200)
Year 3		
Revenue	$381,924	$458,309
Expenses	($159,135)	($254,616)
Year 4		
Revenue	$393,382	$472,058
Expenses	($163,909)	($262,254)
Year 5		
Revenue	$405,183	$486,220
Expenses	($168,826)	($270,122)
Year 6		
Revenue	$417,339	$500,806
Expenses	($173,891)	($278,226)
NPV	$23,420	($60,405)

year six, however, only property #1 has a positive NPV. If we anticipate being in the deal for less than six years, our NPV will be negative, indicating that we won't be generating the 10 percent discount rate on the cash outlay.

Essentially this tells us that if we have an alternative investment that *will* generate the 10 percent we are looking for, we should choose it instead of investing in this property. Notice that this analysis shows a higher NPV for property #1, where the ratio of expenses to income is lower.

NPV gives us what we need in order to calculate (Figure 8) our *internal rate of return* (IRR). Investors are often used to focusing on the IRR for a deal. In our NPV example, we used a 10 percent discount rate, which yielded a positive NPV over seven years. But what if we just want to know what the rate of return is at breakeven?

Let's say I have a choice between two investments (in this case the two comparison properties) and I want to know which one is likely to generate the higher return. Or maybe I want to decide whether I should be investing in

---

Figure 8: INTERNAL RATE OF RETURN (IRR) FORMULA

$$\textbf{IRR} = r, \text{ when}$$

$$\textbf{NPV} = \sum_{t=0}^{N} \frac{C_t}{(1+r)^t} = 0$$

---

real estate at all and I am going to compare my returns to those I would expect when buying stocks or treasuries—some alternative investment which we can use as a baseline for our comparison.

The idea with IRR is that you want the NPV of all the cash flows to zero out so you have an *apples to apples* comparison. Essentially, you are estimating the chances that one deal will generate returns greater than those you will get with another.

With IRR, we take these cash flows and figure out, at what interest rate will you equal your initial investment? The higher the rate, the better the investment. In fact, investment companies often have an established *hurdle rate*, which indicates the threshold at which they are willing to invest.

Figure 9: EXAMPLE: IRR

	Prop #1	Prop #2
Year 1		
Revenue	$360,000	$432,000
Expenses	($1,200,000)	($1,290,000)
Year 2		
Revenue	$370,800	$444,960
Expenses	($159,135)	($254,616)
Year 3		
Revenue	$381,924	$458,309
Expenses	($163,909)	($262,254)
Year 4		
Revenue	$393,382	$472,058
Expenses	($168,826)	($270,122)
Year 5		
Revenue	$405,183	$486,220
Expenses	($173,891)	($278,226)
Year 6		
Revenue	$417,339	$500,806
Expenses	($179,108)	($286,573)
IRR	**10.33%**	**5.60%**

(I have encouraged you to use a target margin for your distressed property investment in the same way. If you can earn that margin or greater, the deal falls within an acceptable range. If not, walk away.)

Again, my example (Figure 9) uses Excel to calculate IRR based on the same data we used to calculate NPV.

It is common for investors to try to maximize their investment by reinvesting the positive cash flows and plowing them back into the investment for the duration of its term.

In order to account for the additional compounding this approach represents, you will need to modify the IRR calculation. This new calculation is called, not surprisingly, the *modified internal rate of return* (MIRR).

This example (Figure 10) shows the MIRR. Notice the differ-

Figure 10: EXAMPLE: MODIFIED IRR (MIRR)

	Prop #1	Prop #2
Year 1		
Revenue	$360,000	$432,000
Expenses	($1,200,000)	($1,290,000)
Year 2		
Revenue	$370,800	$444,960
Expenses	($159,135)	($254,616)
Year 3		
Revenue	$381,924	$458,309
Expenses	($163,909)	($262,254)
Year 4		
Revenue	$393,382	$472,058
Expenses	($168,826)	($270,122)
Year 5		
Revenue	$405,183	$486,220
Expenses	($173,891)	($278,226)
Year 6		
Revenue	$417,339	$500,806
Expenses	($179,108)	($286,573)
MIRR	10.19%	7.42%

ence between MIRR and our previous IRR example. Now that property #2 is able to reinvest its larger cash flows, it is a much more competitive investment in relation to property #1.

Predicting the complete future by plugging numbers into statistical models, however complex, is impossible. It is important to remember that there is a fuzzy crystal ball element to all valuations. We are using a set of tools, each of which has its inherent limitations, in order to predict future performance. The closest we can get is to model the past and establish the most reasonable probability for what is to come. By using multiple analyses, you can increase your chances of seeing the deal from all angles and detecting pitfalls and risks not apparent on the surface.

All of these exercises are aimed at increasing your understanding of what is reasonable in terms of the market price for your investment property. Use the tools at your disposal to obtain your best understanding of what the property's true current market value (your ARV) is before you decide to submit an offer.

Contract and Close

CHAPTER TWENTY-ONE

How Much to Offer?

Whether you are focused on pre-foreclosure properties, bidding at a foreclosure auction, or bidding on REO properties, your preparation is critical. You should know exactly what you are prepared to offer and why.

If you have selected only properties that fit your profile and which fit with your financing options and taken the time and effort to perform thorough due diligence, you are ready to prepare your bidding criteria. You will see this sentiment repeated throughout this book: You make your money in distressed property investing by buying right! The next step is establishing your criteria for bids that will give you the greatest chance of a return on your investment.

Jumping into this step unprepared is a quick way to take losses. Believe me, I have submitted offers and then discovered a nasty problem while the offer was being considered. You do not want to be in the position I was in—hoping that your offer is rejected because you missed a critical element during due diligence.

I'm sure some of you will be reading this and thinking, "If I had only read this book sooner—I am in that exact situation right now!" My only advice if this is where you find yourself is to take a close look and see if taking the loss of your earnest money is less painful than getting embroiled in a deal that could ruin you. As a general rule, your first loss is your best loss.

> *Inexperienced buyers often fall into the trap of becoming motivated themselves*

If the market will only yield a certain price for any given property, it stands to reason that the opportunity to increase the margin is in the buying more than in the selling. This makes submitting the right offer the critical step, since the offer is your real opportunity to capture whatever margin is available in the property. Let's start looking at offers by identifying what can keep you from submitting the right offer.

Warren Buffet is quoted as saying, "Once you have ordinary intelligence, what you need is the temperament to control the urges that get other people into trouble in investing."[21] Disciplining yourself to avoid making emotional decisions that could cost you money starts right from the beginning.

As we stated earlier, the reason for the opportunity in distressed real estate starts with a motivated seller, the banks and lenders. Inexperienced buyers often fall into the trap of becoming motivated themselves. They develop an emotional attachment or become enamored with the possibilities that the investment represents. They step into the shoes of a retail home buyer rather than an investor.

Remember: You aren't picking up a puppy at the Humane Society; you are investing and creating value by operating as a part of the real estate market.

Investing is not about whether your furniture would look great in this floor plan, or whether you could get used to looking out at that view every day.

You need to develop the discipline to follow your game plan and be willing to walk away if the deal does not meet the terms you outlined in your profile. Do not waste time trying to justify purchasing a property if the numbers are bad. Develop the habit of setting your emotions aside and evaluating properties objectively. There is no squeezing a round peg into a square hole in this business. If it doesn't fit, walk away.

If there is one lesson that will help keep you from getting burned, it is that *there is always another deal*.

Another emotional problem you might encounter is the *reaction* to your offer. Realtors and bank sellers may thrash around and flagellate themselves about how offensive your low-ball offer is. You should be prepared to show a rationale why you think the offer makes sense, but also do not get hung up on the emotions at work with the other party across the negotiating table.

As I mentioned earlier, if you are using a Realtor, make sure he or she is not afraid of submitting a low bid. Their fiduciary obligations state that they *must* submit all offers, but if you sense friction over the amount of your bid, you might as well save yourself the headaches—just get another Realtor.

Part of the reason making an offer can be so emotional is that new investors are not used to making these deals, so the very first deals have a lot riding on them. If your offer is too low, your offer might not be accepted. If your offer is too high, you leave profit on the table and potentially expose yourself to greater risk.

In our company, we have a fairly sophisticated process for determining what we are willing to offer. The process removes any emotional component and allows us to focus on the specifics of the deal. Because we are evaluating hundreds of properties at a time, we never get hung up on any single property. If a deal has elements that make it more risky, that does not always mean that we will pass, but we expect the bidding price to reflect the increased risk.

Banks typically attempt to establish the fair market value (FMV) of their REO properties using what is called a broker price opinion (BPO), which means they have hired a Realtor to tell them what the property is worth. They do this for two reasons. First, they are not skilled at doing this work themselves—paying a fee to the Realtor is a transaction they understand. And second, they have an obligation to their shareholders to make their best efforts to protect the cash in the bank. By using a third-party Realtor to perform this service, they are covering their base in case anyone scrutinizes their efforts.

The problem is that the Realtors hired to perform the BPOs are getting paid by the banks. Even though fees for BPOs typically only run from $50 to $150, Realtors often feel an obligation to deliver good news. As a result, they often return optimistic opinions and overvalue these properties. So, you have banks who think the property is worth more than it is, and Realtors listing properties at prices that have less chance of selling.

In order to combat this, you need to establish the value yourself and be prepared to justify it to the bank. Your best chance of getting the bank to accept a lower offer is to thoroughly justify your position. Take pictures, find comparables, and do not forget that the market is not static. Values are moving targets. If the market is falling and the BPO was done a couple of months ago, the property could have dropped in value 2 to 8 percent, a significant impact on your bottom line if you pay too much, but also a reality the bank must acknowledge if they hope to move the property.

Banks are fickle, but their responses to your offer will generally fall into one of four buckets: They may reject your offer, they may counter your offer, they may reject it and give you an opportunity to counter, or they may accept. There is perhaps a fifth option (which is really a rejection) which is somewhat more frustrating for you as the investor—that is, the *ignore play*. You may submit a bid and hear nothing at all. No matter what the outcome, you want to take your best shot and provide as much information supporting your offer as you can.

Many of my recommendations this far have indicated this, but just to underscore the importance, I will say it again. Before making an offer, (especially first-time) investors you ought to make every effort to thoroughly understand the property's *actual* value. This means its value to the market, not necessarily its value to you.

Unless you want to end up owning the property yourself, you need to know how quickly you can turn it, and that means a sale to someone on the open market. If you first do your homework and spend some *shoe leather* looking at similar homes on the market, you will be much more confident in your bid.

Take advantage of terms that may make your offer more attractive such as paying all cash, or emphasizing your capability to close quickly.

Develop a systematic method for calculating your bids. For example, a common approach that I recommend is to start with your ARV, multiply by 70 percent and subtract your repair costs. This should yield your *maximum* bid.

ARV x .70 - Repairs = **Max Bid**

For example, if you have done your homework, estimated an ARV of $250,000 (assuming that the property will sell within 30 DOM, a time frame which you feel is acceptable), with $25,000 in repairs required, you would calculate your bid as follows.

ARV	$250,000
70%	$175,000
Repairs	($25,000)
Maximum Bid	**$150,000**

You are free to tweak this process for your needs. However, I caution you against tweaking it in a way that shrinks your margins. If the deal doesn't have enough money in it to make it worth your while, ask yourself whether or not you should be doing it.

Use the same process for every deal in order to maintain an *apples to apples* comparison. If you cannot get the numbers to add up, it is best to pass on the deal.

CHAPTER TWENTY-TWO

Liens

Real property is used to secure many types of obligation—the most common of these is a mortgage. The instrument securing these obligations to the property is called a lien and represents an *encumbrance* on the title of the property. There are two types of liens: Voluntary (also called statutory or non-consensual liens) and involuntary (also called equitable or consensual).[22]

Mortgages are considered voluntary liens because the borrower entered into the mortgage agreement voluntarily. An example of an involuntary lien is a mechanic's lien filed by a contractor for work performed on the property or a tax lien filed by the government.

In customary practice, a lien makes property difficult to sell, because the new owner does not want any dispute over the ownership of the property and title companies do not want to insure titles that have potential claims against them or *clouds* over them. I say customary because liens in and of themselves do not typically restrict the sale of the property, but they may restrict things like the new buyer's ability to get title insurance, or the new buyer's ability to use the property as collateral. It is possible to bond around liens that are in the process of being worked out, but in general, you want to avoid unnecessary liens.

Liens can originate from several sources, and the order or priority in which they have a right to be repaid is called their *position*. A common way to look at this is a home with a first and second mortgage on it.

The first mortgage is in *first position* on the property. That means that if the lien is foreclosed in order to produce a sale of the property and satisfy the lien, any proceeds from the sale go to the lien in first position initially, then any balance goes to the lien in second position, and so on.

Lien holders, or lienees, are very concerned about the position of their lien because if the proceeds of a sale are not sufficient to cover all liens with greater priority than theirs, they are left with a debt that is unsecured and therefore virtually uncollectible.

Liens can be filed against a property by the government, banks and lenders, contractors (as in my example of mechanic's liens), homeowners' associations (HOAs) and practically anyone who claims an interest in the property. (Many states have enacted harsh penalties for wrongful liens as a deterrent from people filing frivolous liens. Consult with your real estate attorney regarding statutes in the area in which you plan to invest.)

A foreclosure affects liens. For example, liens for property taxes are typically required to be brought current by the seller at closing regardless of the foreclosure (more about these liens in the next section). Mechanic's liens and subordinate (i.e., lower in priority) liens, however, are wiped out in a foreclosure. The mortgage lien itself is typically the subject of the foreclosure and the bank resolves it through the process of foreclosure.

Since most liens are subordinate to a first mortgage, it is easy to think that you might not have to worry about them at all. Be careful that an exception doesn't surprise you. What you need to watch out for are liens that have the ability to penetrate the foreclosure. Liens that persist after you have purchased the property *will become your responsibility* and could be very problematic.

> *What you need to watch out for are liens that might penetrate the foreclosure*

An example of a lien that could persist even after foreclosure might be an lien placed by an HOA. Properties that are part of an HOA are bound by the covenants, conditions and restrictions (CC&Rs) or bylaws within the association. These CC&Rs are recorded against the title of all the member properties, typically when they are first constructed with subsequent amendments being recorded along the way.

HOAs are typically funded by the dues paid by the members—the property owners in the association. When those dues go unpaid, the HOA then has the right, according to the terms written into the CC&Rs or bylaws, to place a lien on the property. These liens can persist through a foreclosure, so you need to discover them before you close.

You can find all liens and encumbrances recorded against a property through a title search. A title search is one area where you may want to consider paying a professional. If you have enlisted a title company as part of your investment advisory team, this is where they assist you. If you haven't identified someone to help yet, now may be the time to find a professional *title abstractor* to do the title search for you.

CHAPTER TWENTY-THREE

Taxes

The government always gets its share. Tax liens are *always* in first position on a property's title. This is a concern for distressed property investors because the same economics that cause borrowers to default on their mortgages can cause them to be delinquent in paying their property taxes.

Banks typically protect themselves against this in single-family home mortgages by setting up an escrow account and collecting money every month for taxes and insurance, along with the mortgage payment. However, when borrowers default, money stops flowing into that account. If the process of foreclosure takes several months, or the house has been on the market for some time, money for taxes quickly runs out and by the time the property comes to you, taxes are likely to be an issue.

Transfer of title often requires that taxes be brought current. In most cases property taxes are only paid once a year, but the pro rata portion of the taxes due based on when during the year the sale takes place is generally paid by each party at closing. The purchase contract will typically address who is responsible for bringing taxes current (customarily the seller).

That does not mean that, as the seller, a bank won't try to pull something over on you. When it comes to who pays the taxes, make sure you know if it is you! Don't find yourself wiped out at closing when the funds you anticipated as profits get siphoned off to pay taxes.

> *Don't find yourself wiped out at closing when the funds you anticipated as profits get siphoned off to pay taxes*

Investment properties also impact your bottom line through other types of taxes. If you are new to investing or property ownership, you may also be new to capital gains taxes. As you anticipate selling an investment property, make sure you consult with an accountant (preferably the one you have recruited to your investment advisory team) and understand the implications of capital gains taxes on your anticipated returns.

Similarly, if you have never owned rental property before, you may not be aware of the tax shelter benefits of depreciating the improvements on income property. Tax benefits can sometimes be so significant that they provide the entire motivation for a buyer.

CHAPTER TWENTY-FOUR

Creating a Holding Company

I always recommend that investment properties be purchased in the name of a company created for the purpose of holding the property, rather than personally. This simply requires that you form a company to act as the buyer in the transaction. Your attorney should be able to help you file the necessary paperwork with the Department of Commerce in your state.

Why take the extra step and incur the hassle and expense of forming a company for the transaction? I highly recommend that you consult with the real estate attorney on your investment advisory team regarding all of the benefits of forming a company as well as the benefits of the various types of business entities. But essentially, a company provides protection for you from liability.

In the worst case, a bad deal could end up in a lawsuit for any number of reasons. By forming a holding company, your risks are generally limited to your exposure in the company.

In other words, as an individual (i.e., self-proprietor) you bear unlimited and unseverable personal liability for any claims that arise from the deal. That means that if you lose a lawsuit over something related to the deal, it is possible that you would not only lose the house you planned to invest in, *but you could lose the one you are living in!*

The net effect is that you could lose not only the dollars you have invested in this deal, but the dollars you have *anywhere* else as well. A company essentially creates a barrier that limits your liability (in most cases) to what you have in the company. You do not want one bad deal to spread to your other deals.

CHAPTER TWENTY-FIVE

Financing

The common logic is that REO properties are only available to buyers coming to the table with cash. This is probably a misconception that comes from trustee sales, sheriff sales and auctions, which require a cashier's check on the spot and the remainder within 24 hours.

I am a little wary of discussing alternatives to cash, because cash truly is king. Cash is certainly the strongest position for negotiation, and offers you the best chance to get the most attractive deal. But is just is not true that all foreclosures are sold for cash.

Back at the beginning, I recommended that you review your financing strategy as part of your investment profile. When it comes to executing that financing strategy, your goal is to avoid letting your financing become an issue for the seller—i.e., the lender. If you can still produce the funds, timely and without excuses, you should be able to execute the sale.

Just remember, the banks are motivated by the opportunity to get that money quickly and get it back into their lending pool. They will not be inclined to haggle about your lack of ability to perform. Do not take the risk of both losing a good opportunity and falling out of favor with the banks. Nothing creates a bad impression like having a deal go bad when it is your fault. Make sure you have explored your options and secured your financing before you begin negotiating with banks or property owners.

Sometimes, you can negotiate with the bank to finance your purchase of an REO they are listing. This is tricky, because you are letting them have some control over both sides of the deal, but I have seen buyers successfully negotiate with banks who desperately needed to convert the non-performing REO assets into standard, performing assets on their books. In the end, the most important factor is that the bank is willing to sell at a price that fits your profile. So long as that is in place, it doesn't matter what the bank's motivation is.

CHAPTER TWENTY-SIX

Negotiating and Submitting Your Bid

Banks typically have a department responsible for negotiating with buyers in distress, approving short sales, and the disposition of their REO property. Although each bank is different, this is often the loan loss mitigation department for properties in pre-foreclosure, and the home loan trading group or the capital markets group for the disposition of REO properties.

I recommend that you always make every effort to try to contact the lender directly. You want to speak with the head of the department. Get to the head of the home loan trading department or whatever department handles the sale of assets (or asset management) for the bank's REOs. Explain that you want to view and possibly make an offer on the property. The head of this department is also who you want to submit your offer or bid to.

The first step is often submitting a *Letter of Intent* or LOI. Your LOI is really just a way to tell the bank that you are interested in the property. It is a placeholder that the bank might use as it decides what to do with its REOs. If the bank knows that you are interested, they may contact you. Otherwise, this step is simply throwing your hat in the ring and telling the bank that you understand the process. It may not mean much in terms of whether or not your bid is accepted, but it gives you an opportunity to make contact and begin developing that critical relationship with the players that you may come to depend on.

Next, you submit your bid or offer. If you have chosen to add a Realtor to your investment advisory team, the offer should be submitted through them. Otherwise, you should represent that you are the buyer and are acting without an agent.

You should plan on your offer including an earnest money of typically 10 percent of the purchase price (see the next section for more about earnest monies) and the bank may require you to prove that you are capable of making the purchase. They do this by requesting Proof of Funds similar to what is required in order to participate in the public foreclosure auction. They require this as a way of shaking out real buyers from the Lookie Lous—people who shop only to satisfy their curiosity, waste a seller's time and never buy.

One of the challenges investors find is that it is often difficult to get lenders to deal with them directly. If the bank has listed its REO properties with a real estate broker, they may want to require that contact and offers are made through the Realtor.

There is also an industry of middle men that you may encounter. They are called intermediaries, seller's mandates, or seller's agents, etc. These players are trying to earn a split of the commission on the sale of the properties and often claim that they have exclusive authority to represent the seller, whether or not this is really true.

As a general rule, make every effort to reach out to the bank, the seller, itself. Intermediaries—even legitimate real estate professionals—just tend to get in the way of getting a deal done. If you absolutely cannot penetrate to the seller, make every effort to get as close as possible. In other words, the closer you can get to the seller, the better your chances of having your offer fairly represented.

Regardless of its experience in real estate, the lender will very likely be skilled at negotiation—which means that many times they won't negotiate at all.

If you get to the point that they will accept your offer, and you are negotiating on certain points of the purchase contract the bank will be represented by its attorney. (Banks often have their attorneys draft their purchase contracts for them.) You should be prepared for negotiations to be conducted between your real estate attorney and the bank's attorney after your offer is submitted. This negotiation could go back and forth right up until the purchase contract is signed.

Once you sign, you are on the hook. Technically, many states have a *buyer's remorse* grace period in which home purchases can be voided. Consult with your real estate attorney to determine whether or not this applies to your situation.

However, my point remains that you need to know your position going in, before you submit an offer, before you enter any type of negotiations, and definitely before you execute a contract. The bank's representatives will not show weakness in their position, even if both of you know it exists. You should be prepared to walk away from a deal, even if the only thing wrong with it is the banker's attitude.

Remember, emotions make for bad deals. Always be willing to walk away.

You should also be prepared for the fact that, unlike individual sellers, banks sellers will most often not perform repairs (although some asset managers have done this), or allow contingencies in the purchase contract that depend upon inspection. It is possible to get inspection and repair provisions into the deal, but where this is quite common in the retail market, it is uncommon with REOs.

You should expect very little wiggle room. The property will most likely come to you *as-is* so you need to have done your due diligence ahead of time and be fully aware of what you are getting into.

Any response contact from the bank after you submit your bid is typically a good sign. A response means at least you are not getting the ignore play, truly a favorite among banks and lenders. If you have not successfully made your case that your bid is fair, or for any of a host of other reasons your bid does not fit their criteria, you will be flatly rejected, if contacted at all.

If you submitted a bid based upon your profile and your understanding of the property's true value, you have given it your best shot. If your offer still gets rejected—better luck next time. Expect this to happen on deals. I do not know anyone who has been in this business a significant length of time who does not have a hefty stack of rejections. If you think you will struggle with constant and repeated rejection, you might want to reconsider getting into this type of investing. Persistence is the name of the game.

If your offer is interesting to the bank, you might get a response that sounds something like this,

"We are currently considering multiple offers and the running is tight. Please present your *highest and best* offer."

This is a common response whether there are any other offers on the table or not. If you can afford to give a little, that might be all it takes to get the deal. Just remember, that if it does not meet your profile, you are better off to walk away.

CHAPTER TWENTY-SEVEN

The REPC

My father always told me "your word is your bond and your handshake is a contract, but if you do not get it in writing, it's worthless."

Legally, all transfers of real property must be in writing. Although property could be sold with a simple bill of sale or even given away with a quit claim deed, the document that typically describes the terms of this transaction is a *real estate purchase contract* or REPC. In some states, Realtors are required by law to only use state-approved REPC forms, including state-approved addenda. In others, REPCs simply must contain all of the provisions legally required.

The REPC will outline the terms of the sale. I always recommend that you retain a skilled and experienced real estate attorney to draft these contracts, along with any addenda. I recommend against cookie-cutter contracts. These are typically drafted only to limit litigation, where a document prepared by your own attorney has a much better chance of representing your interests.

> **"** *I recommend against cookie-cutter contracts* **"**

You may initially have an aversion to the cost of hiring an attorney. I strongly encourage you to develop a good relationship with an attorney particularly skilled in real estate for two reasons: First, if you are serious about making your living investing in real estate, you ought to consider this an essential role in your team of professional investment advisors; second, the financial consequences of legal mistakes can be devastating—a good attorney is like insurance against inexperienced mistakes that can wipe you out. I have been in this business a long time, and I would not be without my attorney in any of my deals.

You should be familiar with the elements contained in a typical REPC. REPCs will list the buyer and seller, contain a description of the property, include terms relating to financing, condition of the property, condition of title, provisions for default by buyer and seller, terms of possession, and terms regarding the Earnest Money. The REPC often also requires disclosures from the seller as to the condition of the property.

Earnest money is essentially a deposit, which is refundable under certain conditions and nonrefundable under others. Real estate brokers keep a trust account for holding earnest monies. It is typical for banks to accept 10 percent of the purchase price as earnest money on REO properties. Although it is possible for lenders to require more or less, 10 percent is customary. Note that this is much higher than the amount of earnest money typically required on retail home sales. This increase reflects the commitment that banks expect to see before they waste time on buyers that cannot perform.

If your offer is accepted, the bank will probably present you with a REPC as a counter to your offer that describes the terms as they want to see them. You should be prepared to thoroughly review this. Do not sign it unless you understand and accept all the terms.

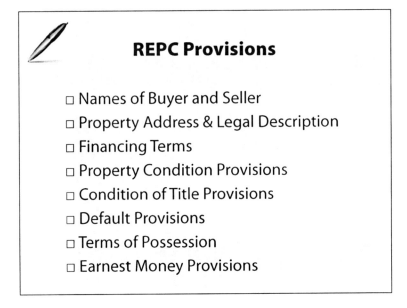

REPC Provisions

□ Names of Buyer and Seller
□ Property Address & Legal Description
□ Financing Terms
□ Property Condition Provisions
□ Condition of Title Provisions
□ Default Provisions
□ Terms of Possession
□ Earnest Money Provisions

In our company, because we make it a practice to submit an extensive due diligence file substantiating the value of our bid, we typically submit offers that include a *fade* provision. A fade provision means we intend to justify a lower price as our due diligence indicates is fair. The bank does not have to accept the fade, of course, but having it in the contract gives us greater flexibility when it comes to finalizing the contract at a price we want to pay. Once the terms are in a contract that has been accepted, both parties can work within those terms without starting back at square one.

CHAPTER TWENTY-EIGHT

Closing, Title and Escrow

Once you have a REPC signed by both you and the bank, the next step is closing. Closing, or *settlement* is when the contract is fulfilled and the official transfer of property ownership from the seller to the purchaser takes place. Technically, there can be a few days after signatures are executed in which title can be recorded, financing can still fund, and other details can take place, but for all intents and purposes the sale is completed at closing.

Closing itself typically happens at the offices of a title company and often involves a lot of paperwork and a lot of signatures.

As an investor, you can prepare for the closing process by understanding what you need to have ready in order to close. Being prepared will make the entire process smoother and less stressful.

Surprises that arise at closing are not fun for anyone involved.

The following steps are typical. However, keep in mind that real estate settlement laws and requirements vary from state to state.

Often prior to closing, you will go through a pre-settlement checklist.

You must have your financing lined up. If you are securing a loan as part of your purchase, you must have a loan approval in place prior to closing. In fact, the POF may require that you have all of your financing in place earlier in the process than would be required if you were making a traditional purchase instead of buying an REO. The POF could mean that your loan has not only been approved, but has funded and the proceeds are ready and available to you.

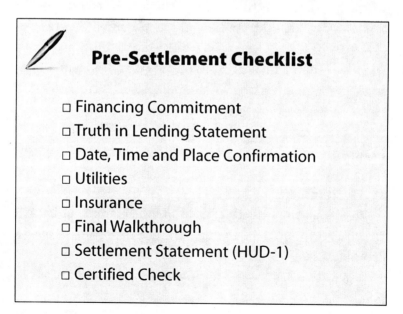

Pre-Settlement Checklist

- ☐ Financing Commitment
- ☐ Truth in Lending Statement
- ☐ Date, Time and Place Confirmation
- ☐ Utilities
- ☐ Insurance
- ☐ Final Walkthrough
- ☐ Settlement Statement (HUD-1)
- ☐ Certified Check

If you are financing part of the purchase, your lender will provide you with a Truth-In-Lending statement. The Truth-In-Lending statement outlines the loan repayment terms, including the total cost of the loan, if you follow the anticipated repayment schedule, including principal and interest. This is the point at which first-time home buyers are shocked and horrified to learn that their $100,000 home is actually costing them $350,000!

Remember to confirm the date, time and place of closing—this is an appointment you don't want to miss. It is not uncommon for banks to want to close at the offices of the title company where they do most of their business. They have typically negotiated more favorable fees due to the volume of work represented by their account. The confirmation represents agreement between the lender (if any), the title/escrow company, and the buyer and seller.

Utilities are sometimes neglected and become an irritation. You should transfer utility accounts into the name of your holding company prior to closing. It is a good idea to reinspect that all utility-impacted systems in the property are working properly as part of your final walkthrough. Remember to get them transferred out of your responsibility after you sell. (We have had many buyers enjoy complimentary power and heating for a few months in cases where our staff failed to notice this detail. Of course, none of our buyers were upset at this being overlooked by our team.)

Just like with auction properties, you ought to be prepared to have the property insured from the moment you own it.

Most lenders will require homeowners, hazard & liability insurance as a condition of the loan. Even if you are executing the deal in cash and expect a quick sale, do not take the risk that something could happen to the property during that period. This is simply a common-sense protection of your investment.

You should also know whether or not flood insurance is required. Check out *http://www.floodsmart.gov* or other resources to determine if the property is located in a flood plain. It is often helpful to know if flood insurance has been carried on the property before.

Typically sellers allow buyers to make a final walk-through inspection a day or two before closing. This is your last chance to view the property before taking ownership of it. Make sure everything is as you remember it (no new damages).

Also, if you were successful in making the contract contingent upon certain repairs, make sure the seller actually completed those repairs. Although your earnest money could be at risk, if you find problems during the final walk-through, you are still free to back out of the deal. Losing your earnest money may be preferable to losing your shirt.

At least one business day before settlement, you should receive a settlement statement (also referred to as a HUD-1 statement). This document will list all the costs you are required to pay at closing. Review it carefully. If you find errors or items you do not understand, bring it up with your real estate agent, attorney or settlement agent.

In most cases, you will need to bring a certified check with you to settlement to cover all the closing costs for which you are responsible. The amount of this check is based on the settlement statement. (Be sure to bring a government-issued photo ID with you as well. Title companies are required to verify the identities of the parties to the transaction.)

Losing your earnest money may be preferable to losing your shirt

Assuming all things are in order, at closing, your will be required to sign documents and make payment of the purchase price and cover your portion of closing costs and title/escrow fees.

If you are getting a loan and have not signed your loan documents prior to closing, you will be required to sign them at closing. This is unusual, but not unheard of when purchasing an REO property.

These documents represent the agreement between you and your lender regarding the terms and conditions of the mortgage. The remaining documents represent the agreement between you and the seller transferring ownership of the property. Again, be sure to read all documents carefully before signing them, and do not sign forms with blank lines or spaces.

Title companies sometimes make jokes about this type of buyer—one who is a *reader*—because most retail buyers do not take the time to read the mountain of paperwork presented to them at closing. You may have felt the same way when you purchased your first home. However, you owe it to yourself to read and understand everything that could potentially impact your investment.

Typically, after signing all the appropriate documents and paying the closing costs, the title company, escrow agent or attorney will record in the county recorder's office all documents such as the warranty and security deeds, return to the lender the completed loan package, and disburse all funds in accordance with the HUD-1 settlement statement.

If you bought the property in a foreclosure auction, however, you will receive the deed immediately and it will be your responsibility to take it to the county recorder's office or the register of deeds and get it recorded in your name.

Once you own the property, the clock is ticking. The faster you can turn the property from the time you buy it until your desired exit, the greater your chances for return on your investment and the less you end up paying in various holding costs like insurance, utilities, and taxes.

The nature of REOs often means these properties have taken a beating. In Chapter 17, "Rehab Estimates," we discussed how essential it is to be able to estimate rehab costs as part of your due diligence and evaluate which repairs will bring the greatest ROI. In this following section, "Rehabilitation," we will discuss more about how to get the work done.

One of the cheapest and most valuable things you can add to a property is soap and water. A good cleaning will do wonders.

Beyond that, superficial cosmetic repairs and refurbishment (often called *lipstick*) like fresh paint and new carpeting can generate great returns yet keep your costs low. Typically, if you need to install carpet or anything more involved, you will need to get outside help; you will need to find a contractor.

Rehabilitation

CHAPTER TWENTY-NINE

Finding a Contractor

Contractors, like Realtors, run the gamut from trusted professionals to crooks. As a newbie, you cannot afford to choose the wrong one.

A good contractor is an indispensable resource for your REO investing. Finding a good contractor requires a little homework. To start with, set up a competitive bidding process, where you request bids (for more complex work, this could be a request for proposals, i.e., RFP) from multiple contractors on the same scope of work. It is important that you understand and outline the scope of work ahead of time. Scope creep is one of the quickest ways to lose your shirt in real estate investing.

Interview contractors like you would your daughter's prom date. Do not be afraid to probe and ask a lot of questions. Watch for signs of dishonesty. Do they look you in the eyes? Do they talk about getting ripped off? Are they complainers? I find that contractors who constantly com-

Contractor Checklist

Request Competitive Bids from Multiple Contractors!

Ensure Contractors Provide

- ☐ Active License in Good Standing
- ☐ Insurance (Bond if Necessary)
- ☐ Evidence of Good Standing with BBB and Trade Associations
- ☐ Multiple Trade References
- ☐ A Clean "Google"

Protect Yourself

- ☐ Contract for a "Guaranteed Maximum Price" (GMP)
- ☐ Establish a Firm Timeline with Delay Penalties
- ☐ Review the Contract with Your Attorney
- ☐ Ensure You Have Included the Entire Scope of Work
- ☐ Thoroughly Discuss the Process for Change Orders
- ☐ Understand Your Risk of Mechanic's Liens

plain about previous jobs, or the contractor who performed work ahead of them, or contract terms, etc., typically have trouble being completely and fairly responsible for completing their own work. You want someone who will get the job done, not come up with excuses why they couldn't.

Ask every bidder to go back and sharpen his pencil. It is okay for contractors to make a fair profit, but ensuring that happens is not your responsibility. After you have asked each of your bidders if that is their best price, review the estimates and begin doing some due diligence on the contractors themselves.

Hiring a private detective to do background checks on the contractor on your list for consideration might be a little excessive, but there is some basic detective work you can and should do on your own. Make these steps a habit whenever you are getting ready to contract for rehab or remodel work.

General contractors and subcontractors in most trades are licensed by the state in which they operate. If your state requires a license for the type of work you are getting done, make sure you check with the state licensing board and verify that your contractor has a license and that it is in good standing.

Check with the consumer protection agency and the attorney general's office in your state to see if any complaints have been filed.

Typically, contractors are limited in the size of the jobs that they can take, based upon the amount of insurance they carry. License and insurance details should be items contractors are showing potential customers all the time. Ask to see them and keep a copy for your records.

Depending on the type of work and its value, a bond may be required. Make sure the contractor is properly bonded and that the amount of the bond is appropriate considering the cost and scope of the work.

You should also check with the Better Business Bureau or BBB. While the BBB is a private organization and not regulated by the government, they have built a reputation and are a trusted resource for many as well as a place for consumer complaints.

They provide an online search function at *http://www.bbb.org* that is localized and lists individual complaints by consumers. Be sure to search for the name of the contractor as well as any name variations.

In addition to the BBB, many trades are organized into labor unions and professional associations. These organizations are usually interested in promoting the good reputation of their body of members and distancing themselves from bad publicity. If your contractor is in bad standing with the appropriate trade organization, a telephone call will likely reveal it.

Never contract with someone without first requesting references for both customers and business trade relationships and then follow up on them. Find out what type of experience the contractor delivered to others who have already worked with them. Suppliers, bankers used by contractors, and other general contractors in the area will help you understand the reputation of a particular contractor.

Finally, perform an Internet search using Google or another search engine. You may want to add terms to your search that narrow the results down to complaints, problems, and claims of dishonesty.

Watch for entries on sites like Yelp.com, AngiesList.com, or RipoffReport.com which specialize in reporting bad consumer experiences.

A full vetting of your potential contractors does not guarantee that you will never have a bad experience, but you will have a shot at seeing the writing on the wall and increase your probability that this critical role does not eat up all your profits.

In addition to checking up on your contractors, you should plan on adopting some *best practices* approaches to executing your contracts and overseeing the work.

The estimates you received during the bidding process and the final contract for work, may be separate documents. When it comes time to execute a contract, you should let your attorney review it and you should ensure that the terms of the deal have not changed. In the end, the contract, not the estimate, will govern how much you have to pay.

Whenever possible, contract for an explicit scope of work under a guaranteed maximum price (GMP) contract.[23] By using a GMP contract, the contractor takes responsibility for cost overruns beyond the agreed upon maximum price. This does two things: First, you have some legal protection from creeping costs; second, the contractor has an incentive to bid thoroughly and notice potential overruns up front, before work begins.

Another factor you should consider is time. Delays are notorious and costly for REO investors. Establish a time for completion in your contract, and appropriate penalties for delays.

> *Your leverage to get the work completed is a function of how much money you still hold*

Contract work which improves real property generally gives the contractor the right to place a mechanic's lien on the property as security for payment. I recommend you have your attorney draft a lien release form. Every time you pay a contractor, you should require them to sign the form. This is essentially a receipt for what you paid for and a protection against future title problems. I have seen cases where contractors filed liens but were slow to have them removed even after receiving payment and resolving any dispute. A signed lien release is often enough for you to secure a release of the lien yourself.

If you pay a contractor in installments (typically only when the job is large or lengthy), I recommend your contract withhold 10 to 20 percent as the final payment. And final payments should only be made after you perform a thorough inspection, verify that all punch-list items are completed, that you have received signed lien-releases, and that the job is complete to your satisfaction.

Remember that your leverage to get the work completed is a function of how much money you still hold. In my experience, it is always more difficult to get repairs or punch-list items completed if you have already made full payment.

Frequently inspect the progress along the way and do not be afraid to ask questions if something seems wrong. The relationship with your contractor has an element of trust to it, just like any other relationship. But trust is developed over time. Initially, a lot of checkup might seem annoying to your contractor, but then again, it is not the contractor that will lose money if the deal goes south.

Rehab on REO properties has the potential to bring greater returns because of its impact on perceived value. When the buyers come through, they will be perceptive to the overall impression. It will be this impression that leads to the sale, not the accumulation of repair costs. If your repairs do not add to the perceived value, they are not helping your investment returns, no matter what they cost.

It can be difficult to separate your emotional feelings and your rational mind with respect to repairs. You need to be careful to avoid thinking of repairs in terms of how great the property will look when you are finished, or getting hung up on repairs being done the way you would do them for yourself. Remember that repairs are part of the investment, you cannot attach sentimental value yourself that may be meaningless to the eventual buyer.

CHAPTER THIRTY

What You Should or Shouldn't Do Yourself

Often new investors look at rehab and repair work as an opportunity to gain value by doing work themselves. They think that their sweat equity will increase the margins they get when the property sells, because the work "did not cost them anything." While it is possible to do some or all of the work yourself, especially if you have a background as a contractor or tradesperson, it is also a common pitfall.

Work you perform yourself is not really free. Setting aside the time you spend (which at least has an opportunity cost if it takes away from the time you would be spending finding the next deal), repairs have real costs in materials.

Are you sure that your trip to Home Depot will cost you less than a contractor's visit to the local contractor supply yard? Do you have access to the proper equipment to ensure the job is done efficiently? Are you tackling work that has related liability, like plumbing or electrical work? Would a contractor be licensed and insured to perform this work, where you are not? Will your work, even if done correctly, create a liability in the case of future tenants who discover *latent defects* in the property after they move in.

In general, I recommend that beyond cleaning, very minor repairs, and perhaps painting, investors not perform work themselves unless they are true professionals at the type of work that needs to be done. This might require a little soul searching as you examine yourself and honestly reflect on your capabilities. House flippers often have the preconceived notion that the money to be made is all tied up in their own labor, but for true investors, this is just not the case. Just remember that it is always cheapest to get a job done once and done right—preferably by someone other than you.

CHAPTER THIRTY-ONE

Staging and Presentation

Part of preparing a property for sale is staging and presenting it correctly. Presentation truly can be the difference between the house that sells and the house that sits.

Professional home staging experts are often people with a background in interior design or home décor. There are merits to hiring a professional and you will have to make the determination for yourself according to your individual circumstances and investment. However, there are some basic staging principles and concepts that anyone selling a property should understand.

First, think like a buyer. If your property is a single-family home, try driving up to it and imagining yourself as that person or couple who are searching for just the right home. Depending on your market that might mean they are looking to move in right away, or looking to invest themselves. Either way, approach your property as if for the first time.

Start at the street and assess the curb appeal. Look for anything that seems out of place and make notes of anything that might improve the appearance. Maybe a potted plant would just mask that dent in the aluminum siding, maybe the entrance needs some color to attract attention to the features of the door or sidelights. Are there any bits of trash or debris from all the construction that still need to be cleaned up?

As you approach, think about using your senses to understand all of the unseen information being fed into the minds of your prospects. Are there distracting noises or birds chirping? Do you smell fresh-cut grass or animal droppings? When you grasp the front doorknob, does it feel tight and smooth, or is it loose and rickety?

Think about finishing touches like sparing use of houseplants, flowers or fruit bowls. You may want to play some soothing background music during showings. I recommend turning on most, if not all, of the lights in the house and opening blinds, drawing back curtains and letting as much light in as possible. I never want a buyer walking into a dark and gloomy space. It is also a good idea an hour or so before prospects arrive to open the windows for several minutes and let the fresh air in.

Investors often have the advantage over homeowners when it comes to removing their own personality, because they have typically not occupied the property. It is still a good practice to look for *personalization* and remove it. Remember that you aren't trying to show off your taste and style to prospective buyers, you are trying to present a canvas on which they will imprint their own style.

Keep things clean. Watch for spots and smudges on windows; clean scuffs from baseboards and doors. Think about anything prospects might touch. Wipe down door-knobs and cabinet and appliance handles.

Make sure furnishings are minimized to emphasize the space, while helping buyers see themselves living in the home. If your buyers are investors, emphasize how the home will stand up to renters and features designed for easy maintenance.

Don't crowd the prospects. If your Realtor is handling the selling, let them handle it. They will give you a full report after the prospects have left and extra people creates a nervous, claustrophobic environment instead of the relax-ing peaceful atmosphere that attracts buyers.

Exit

CHAPTER THIRTY-TWO

Non-Sale Exits

The disposition of the property is how you get paid. If you make your money buying right, you realize those gains in the selling. All of the work you have done nurturing the investment to this point rests on your ability to exit the investment with your returns intact.

With the property purchased and rehabilitated, now it's time to realize your profits. I am going to outline four typical dispositions. The first three covered in this chapter are non-sale exits: Seller financing (lease to own, etc.), owner occupancy, and income property.

Seller Financing

Typically, an investor would see seller financing as a less than optimal exit. The reason for this is that seller financing is usually a way to create incentives for buyers who are unwilling or unable to complete a sale. If buyers are plentiful, a quick sale is preferred.

Seller financing protracts the relationship between the buyer and the seller, which increases the risk. It does not yield the full return, which also creates risk and limits your opportunities to reinvest.

If rental property is not your primary focus, you are now in the position of acting as a short-term landlord with full property management responsibilities. In other words, you have a new job, which will encroach onto whatever your primary career focus is. This is not usually an optimal situation.

Even with all of the increased headache and risk, this still may be preferable to owning a property you want to sell and nobody wants to buy. Lease payments may offset or completely cover payments you are obliged to make if you financed the purchase of the property or financed any of the rehab work.

Seller financing is an agreement between you as the seller and your buyer. The buyer makes payments directly to you, and you act as the lender. That means that if the buyer defaults, you are now in the position to evict and foreclose on your foreclosure investment property.

Ideally, seller financing should be a bridge to another solution for the borrower. Maybe the borrower needs time to sell off or clear other debts before he or she can qualify for financing on your property. Maybe they are self-employed and need a year or two to demonstrate their income before they can qualify. Maybe they have credit problems that require time to clean up.

Whatever the reason, your goal should be to establish milestones toward financing with a traditional lender. Those milestones should be written into your purchase agreement and failure to hit them could be cause for default. You need to be able to get the property into the hands of someone with the capacity to buy it, and if your initial buyers are not making good faith efforts, you need a way to pursue other buyers.

Owner Occupancy

A perfectly legitimate exit strategy is owner occupancy. This means an investor chooses to move into and live in the house themselves. Often owner occupants are willing to put more work into rehabilitating a property because they intend to be around to realize the sentimental value of a property. They may feel that the *sweat equity* they will be required to put into the property is a good trade-off for the reduced price.

A drawback to owner occupancy is that it does not provide a repeatable investment model. It may help to look at a property you intend to occupy as a perk from your investing job, rather than as an actual investment itself.

Owner occupancy has limitations in terms of its investment characteristics. Discussion around this exit is limited because owner occupancy is not typically an investing or primarily moneymaking disposition of the property.

Income Property

Another common disposition of investment property is to rent it as income property. What is not to like about the perpetual stream of income that grows with inflation while providing a significant tax advantage?

Well, for starters, income properties are more like businesses than investments. If you intend to avail yourself of this type of exit, ask yourself if buying a different type of business would be as appealing. My point is that if you don't want to run a business (any more than you have already been required to just to bring your investment to this point), you should probably consider choosing a different exit.

Investment properties need to be managed; they to be run in order for them to make money. You should be asking yourself if you are ready to be a landlord.

Have you projected detailed financial models for how this business will operate? Do you know what your costs will be? Do you know what the market rents are in your area? Are you familiar with typical vacancy rates in you're area? Do you have a concept and a plan for creating a competitive advantage over other rental properties in your market?

Do you have a plan for performing the maintenance and repairs that tenants will expect? Are you comfortable collecting rent and processing evictions and collections?

Rent a copy of *Pacific Heights* from NetFlix or Block-buster to test your stomach for the risks of being a landlord. I am not looking to discourage you from taking on this challenge—rental income property can be a very rewarding and profitable investment—just trying to provide you with some sobering information in keeping with the theme of helping you go into these deals with your eyes open.

If the thought of being a landlord is scary to you, but the income property returns are attractive, you may want to consider hiring a professional manager or management company. This service is not free, but you may be able to find a scenario where professional management is well worth the cost in avoided headaches and still lets you participate in the investment returns.

Considering professional management from the outset may help you better screen properties that fit an income profile that can support the management cost. You may find that you can increase the efficiency of the dollars you spend on professional management if you hire managers for multiple properties. If these efficiencies are essential to your investment strategy, you need to be considering multiple properties right from the beginning.

Our company holds several income properties as investments—enough so that we formed our own property management company. When it comes to this type of skill set, in my experience, specialists often can outperform generalists and do it in a way that makes the associated costs very affordable.

CHAPTER THIRTY-THREE

Sale

The simplest exit is a sale. In a single transaction, a buyer takes the property off your hands and your investment cashes out. There is something to be said for cashing out immediately. Although the other exits have their merits and can be appropriate given the right timing and circumstances, my preference is always for a straight sale.

You always have the option of selling your property by yourself in a *For Sale by Owner* or FSBO transaction. Owners have the right to represent themselves. However, it is worth discussing the pros and cons of a FSBO versus hiring a professional Realtor.

Certainly if you have added a Realtor to you're investment advisory team, you have already made the decision that the specific experience and expertise that person represents is valuable to you.

The advantages of a FSBO approach are that you do not have to pay any fees to Realtors (you should still expect to have some selling costs, advertising, open houses, etc.). The disadvantages are that you do not have access to all the same tools Realtors use and you may have less expertise selling real estate and less specific knowledge regarding the market you are operating in. This decision is another one of those that requires a little introspection and honest self-assessment of your talents and abilities.

> *My preference is always for a straight sale*

You should be prepared for the fact that your FSBO advertising will attract as many bottom-feeding Realtors as it does prospective buyers (good Realtors get their listings by referrals from satisfied clients, not combing the classifieds). Selling the property yourself, you will still have Realtors coming to you claiming to represent buyers (FSBO really only means you have chosen not to enlist help *selling* the property, but buyers often are represented by Realtors working under an exclusive agency agreement as the buyer's agent). These buyer's agents will want you to agree to pay them a commission before introducing their buyers to you. Technically, these agents have a fiduciary responsibility to act in the best interest of the buyer, but in practice you can expect them to look out for themselves first, and their buyer's second. This means that even if your property is the perfect one for the buyer's needs, don't expect the Realtor to tell their client about your property until after you have agreed to pay a commission.

A note about real estate commissions if you are unfamiliar with how this business works: It is unlawful in most states for commission prices to be set (again check with your real estate attorney for more details about the price-fixing laws that apply to you), but there is often a customary real estate commission in you're area. It is probably somewhere between five and ten percent.

A real estate office typically is headed up by one or more real estate brokers. A broker is licensed at a level above that of a real estate sales agent. Typically, brokers have had to work as sales agents for a period of time or have sold a certain volume of real estate, for example, before they can apply to be licensed as brokers. The individual requirements for your state should be available from the division of real estate or the office responsible for administering and licensing real estate professionals.

Brokers can act alone, but agents are typically required to be affiliated with a broker. Either brokers or agents can be Realtors. Realtor is the name given to real estate professionals who are members of the National Association of Realtors (NAR). Either a broker or an agent could be an effective member of your investment advisory team.

Commissions are generally paid by the seller. A fee equal to a percentage of the sales price is negotiated up front between the seller and the listing agent on behalf of the listing brokerage. Commissions are typically split between the agents and the brokerages.

In the case where a seller lists the property with a Realtor and the buyer is represented by a Realtor, the commissions will be split between four parties: The listing agent, the listing agent's brokerage, the buyer's agent, and the buyer's agent's brokerage. Sometimes commissions are split equitably (25 percent to each party) and sometimes they have made other arrangements among themselves. It is much more common for there to be inequity between brokers and their agents than it is between seller's and buyer's brokerages.

It is not unusual for listing brokerages to split the entire commission in cases where they find a buyer who is not represented by another agent. However, savvy sellers will address this in their listing agreement and ensure that some of that money comes back to them.

So, let's say you decide to use a real estate broker? A good Realtor *can* truly be invaluable—worth every penny of their commission. Unfortunately, as a group, their reputation ranks close to used car salesmen. So how do you find a good one?

Think of your relationship with your realtor like you would any other essential service provider in your life. Did you find your attorney or your doctor by where they ranked in the yellow pages?

You need to do your homework. Talk to their clients and colleagues. Ask them about their track record and request examples of other properties like yours that they have sold in the area. Ask about their certifications and additional credentials. There are several national and regional organizations that provide additional certifications and training for real estate professionals based on various specialties.

You also need to understand the legal relationship you have with your Realtor. As your legal representation, your *agent* in a real estate transaction, Realtors are actually practicing law in a limited and heavily regulated way. They have a fiduciary responsibility to represent your interests. Do not abdicate the responsibilities of your position as the buyer or seller.

Remember that your Realtor works for you, so do not be pressured into a quick sale if you do not think you are getting the best deal. By a quick sale, I mean a sale for less than your listing price. Realtors have been known to pressure sellers as a way of completing more transactions and earning more commissions.

You need to be careful about rejecting offers at the listing price, however. Listing agreements typically contain language that protects the Realtor. A Realtor's worst nightmare is a seller who, after entering into the contract, decides they no longer want to pay a commission and in order to avoid paying, they reject any offer the Realtor presents. Because of this, listing agreements will oblige sellers to pay the real estate commission under certain conditions whether the property actually sells or not. They often include language that obliges the payment of a commission so long as the Realtor produces a *ready, willing, and able* buyer.

Engaging the services of a Realtor means that you need to understand not only your contract with your Realtor, but any contracts they present to you from potential buyers.

Make sure you understand the terms of any contract you sign. (It would be remiss for me not to recommend that you engage the services of a qualified attorney in addition to your Realtor for the purposes of reviewing contracts—I hope this role has already been included in your investment advisory team.) Remember that even though a Realtor is required by law in some states and required by his brokerage in some cases to use standardized forms when making offers on your behalf—forms which are construed to alleviate the burden on the state courts from superfluous lawsuits over real estate transactions and to protect Realtor commissions—that you are *not* restricted to structuring your transaction with the language or terms included on state-approved forms. Write a deal that favors you.

Sometimes a relationship with a Realtor which began with the best of intentions becomes intolerable. Know when it is time to fire your Realtor. Personally, if I ever discover that my Realtor has lied or misled me or someone else about me, I sever the relationship. You need honesty and integrity in the people around you. My advice here is to make sure your expectations are clear and take decisive action if they are not met.

CHAPTER THIRTY-FOUR

Conclusion

Distressed property investing can be a dynamic and exhilarating endeavor. Many investors have been very successful working the process outlined in this book to generate very healthy returns.

I am sincere in saying that shortening the reset of the bloated real estate market depends on facilitating the transfer of foreclosures back into a fair valued market. The volume of those transfers will be the bottleneck for much of the desperately needed economic recovery in the U.S. The current market is offering every indication that foreclosures and the attendant opportunities are on the rise and will be with us for at least the next several years.

In fact, a recent report[24] indicated that about 11 percent of mortgages in the U.S. are in trouble—which represents a seasonally adjusted increase of 3 percent over last year (2008). The 11 percent figure represents 7.9 percent of mortgages that are 30 days or more past due, and 3.3 percent which are already in the process of foreclosure. This is the highest level since these statistics began to be tracked almost 40 years ago.

Like many types of investing, there is a distinct risk and reward correlation when it comes to investing in distressed property. I have made every effort to help you get a realistic perspective of both the challenges and rewards of tackling this exciting facet of real estate investing.

The saying goes, a fool and his money are soon parted. I hope that the tools provided here will help you to "become wise before you get old." Or, in more practical terms, I hope that this material will help you to avoid the pitfalls and traps that can turn a promising career investing in real estate into a nightmare that wreaks havoc with your life.

To those of you ready to tackle the challenges, face the risks, and show your determination, I invite you to join the ranks of successful investors who are filling their role in getting the economy back on track.

If you have read everything this far, thank you for spending your valuable time. The appendix offers many great resources to help you get started. I wish you good luck and greater prosperity as you make foreclosure investing in the new economy a successful part of your life.

Notes and References

1. Freeby50. More on Historical Home Appreciation. http://freeby50.blogspot.com/2008/05/more-onhistorical-home-appreciation.html

2. Wikipedia. McMansions. 2009. http://en.wikipedia.org/wiki/McMansion

3. McKim, Jennifer B. 2009. Forgotten in Foreclosure, Renters Forced to Live in Decaying Homes. *The Boston Globe Online.* http://www.boston.com/business/articles/2009/02/03/forgotten_in_foreclosures_renters_forced_to_live_in_decaying_homes/

4. Casey, Nicholas. 2009. Banker: 'What'd I Do Wrong, Officer?' Cop: 'You've Got Algae In the Pool, Sir': Fearing Blight, a California Town Makes It a Crime to Neglect Foreclosed Homes. *The Wall Street Journal.* May 1, 2009. http://online.wsj.com/article/SB124112509277274533.html

5. Milwaukee Rising Weblog. 2008. http://milwaukeerising.net/wordpress/2008/12/29/city-tags-lenders-with-property-upkeep-duties/

6. AARP Bulletin. 2009. Foreclosures Open Door to Disorder: Vermin, Crooks, Exploit Housing Market Crisis. http://bulletin.aarp.org/yourmoney/personalfinance/articles/foreclosures_open.html

7. Lucier, Thomas J. 2005. *The Pre-Foreclosure Property Investor's Kit: How to make money buying distressed real estate before the public auction.* Wiley Publishing, Indianapolis, IN. p. 186-187

8. Simon, Ruth. 2009. A Short Sale May Not Mean You're Home Free. *The Wall Street Journal.* http://online.wsj.com/article/SB124104990739271023.html

9. Internal Revenue Service, U.S. Department of the Treasury. 2008. http://www.irs.gov/publications/p544/index.html

10. Bischoff, Bill. 2009. Tax Hits on Property Short Sales. *The Wall Street Journal.* http://online.wsj.com/article/SB124104224634570415.html

11. Roberts, Ralph R. with Joe Kraynak. 2007. *Foreclosure Investing for Dummies: Buy and sell foreclosure, pre-foreclosure, and bank-owned properties.* Wiley Publishing, Indianapolis, IN. p. 19

12. Bigger Pockets. How to Find Foreclosure and Pre-Foreclosure Listings. 2009. www.biggerpockets.com/renewsblog/2006/09/01/how-to-find-foreclosure-and-pre-foreclosure-listings/

13. Nolo. Lis Pendens. 2009. http://www.nolo.com/definition.cfm/term/
    BDA664CA-D50E-468E-90A891295A1D404C

14. Note: web links to government foreclosed properties can be found at http://
    www.biggerpockets.com/government-owned-property.html

15. Mortgage News Daily. Where can I find REO Listings? 2009. www.
    mortgagenewsdaily.com/wiki/REO_Database_List.asp

16. Bigger Pockets. Foreclosed Property Management. 2009. http://www.
    biggerpockets.com/foreclosed_property_management.html

17. Bigger Pockets. How to Find Foreclosure and Pre-Foreclosure
    Listings. 2009. www.biggerpockets.com/renewsblog/2006/09/01/
    how-to-find-foreclosure-and-pre-foreclosure-listings/

18. Bigger Pockets. Foreclosed Property Management. 2009. http://www.
    biggerpockets.com/foreclosed_property_management.html

19. National Institute of Building Inspectors. 2009. http://www.nibi.com/

20. Wikipedia. Gross Rent Multiplier. 2009. http://en.wikipedia.org/wiki/
    Gross_Rent_Multiplier

21. Morningstar. Investing Classroom: Stocks 400. 2005.
    http://news.morningstar.com/classroom2/course.
    asp?docId=145104&page=1&CN=COM

22. Orlando, Frankie, and Marsha Ford. 2007. *The Complete Guide to Locating,
    Negotiating, and Buying Real Estate Foreclosures: What Smart Investors
    Need to Know—Explained Simply.* Atlantic Publishing Group, Ocala, FL
    P. 45

23. Business Dictionary. Guaranteed Maximum Price. 2009. http://www.
    businessdictionary.com/definition/guaranteed-maximum-price-GMP.
    html

24. Hagerty, James R. 2009. Overdue Mortgages Increase. *The Wall
    Street Journal.* March 6, 2009. http://online.wsj.com/article/
    SB123630052006746901.html

About the Author

Kirby Cochran is an educator, speaker and thought leader in the field of management and finance. He has been teaching new venture financing and entrepreneurship to graduate students for over a decade. Kirby currently serves as an adjunct professor in the Finance department of the David Eccles School of Business at the University of Utah. He is a prolific writer and has published many articles demystifying the principles behind raising capital successfully for both new ventures and growth firms with established operations.

Kirby is the manager of Castle Arch Opportunity Partners, a series of real estate investment funds specializing in REO acquisition and disposition. Responsible for hundreds of millions of dollars worth of real estate transactions, he has served as the CEO of Castle Arch Real Estate Investment Company for over 5 years.

Heavily involved in growth company financing and management trends over the past twenty-five years, Kirby is a leading expert on capital structure and shareholder value. A veteran of the venture capital industry and a pioneer of emerging approaches to raising capital, Mr. Cochran has led half a dozen investment funds and raised over $1 billion in equity and debt financing across various industry sectors. He has developed a proprietary model for advising companies on growth strategies and accretive financing. Kirby closely consulted and/or participated in the funding of over 100 companies over the length of his career and has extensive experience investing in and developing emerging growth companies.

In his latest series of articles entitled *Leadership Insight*, Mr. Cochran reveals secrets used by entrepreneurs and CEOs to drive growth in their companies. This information has always been difficult and painful for Senior Managers to acquire, found only in the ruthless university of experience and obtained through costly tuition at the school of hard knocks.

Mr. Cochran is a founder of Longview Financial, a boutique investment bank with offices in New York, Chicago, and Newport Beach. Longview specializes in the financing of new ventures. North Point Advisors, the consulting firm founded by Mr. Cochran, advises growth companies on the implementation of the best practices discussed in Leadership Insight for increasing shareholder value.

Appendix

Bank & Lender REO Websites

Note: Several of the major lenders are in the process of being acquired by other banks. For example, Washington Mutual is now part of JP Morgan Chase and Wachovia is part of Wells Fargo. This sector is changing so fast, we cannot claim that this list will be perpetually up to date, and you may need to do some research as entities change, restructure and enter the market.

21st Mortgage Corporation
> *www.21stmortgage.com/web/21stSite.nsf/locating?OpenForm*
> *Search Criteria: State, City, Zip, Price, Bedrooms, Bathrooms, Property Type*

American Home Mortgage
> *re.oomc.com/staticBroker/reProperties.jsp*
> *Search Criteria: State, Zip Code, Price*

Bank Of America
> *bankofamerica.reo.com/search/*
> *Search Criteria: Property Type, County, City, Price, Bedrooms, Baths, and Zip Code*

BB&T
> *www.bbt.com/bbt/applications/specialassets/search.asp*
> *Search Criteria: State, City, County, Price*

Compass Bank
> *www.compassbank.com/appforms/properties/index.jsp*
> *Search Criteria: State, Property Type Price Range*

Countrywide (acquired by Bank of America)
> *www.countrywide.com/purchase/f_reo.asp*
> *Search Criteria: State and City*

GRP Capital
> *www.grpcapital.com/properties/index.php*
> *Search Criteria: State, City, Zip, Price, Agent, Status*

HSBC
> *www.us.hsbc.com/1/2/3/personal/home-loans/properties*
> *Search Criteria: State*

IndyMac Bank
> *http://apps.indymacbank.com/individuals/realestate/search.asp*
> *Search Criteria: Property Type, City, State, Zip, Price, Bedrooms,*
> *Bathrooms*

Integrated Asset Services
> *www.iasreo.com/homesforsale.aspx*
> *Search Criteria: State, Bedrooms, Baths, Price*

JP Morgan Chase
> *mortgage.chase.com/pages/other/co_properties_landing.jsp*
> *Search Criteria: State, County, City, Zip*

M&T Bank (merging with Provident Bankshares Corporation)
> *http://services.mandtbank.com/personal/mortgage/reomort.cfm*
> *Search Criteria: State, City, Price*

Ocwen Financial REO
> *www.ocwen.com/reo/home.cfm*
> *Search Criteria: State, City, Bedrooms, Baths, Square Footage, Price, Prop-*
> *erty Type*

Regions Financial Corporation
> *http://realestate.regions.com/servlet/Ore/ForeclosedPropertySearch.jsp*
> *Search Criteria: State, City, Property Type*

Taylor Bean
> *www.taylorbeanhomes.com/*
> *Search Criteria: State, City, Zip, County, Price, Bedrooms, Baths, Property*
> *Type*

US Bank
> *www.usbankforeclosures.com/*
> *Search Criteria: State, County, Status, Listing Type, City, Zip, Bedrooms,*
> *Baths, Price*

Wachovia (Acquired by Wells Fargo)
> *reo.wachovia.com*
> *Search Criteria: State, City, Zip, County, Bedrooms, Baths, Price, Property*
> *Type*

Washington Mutual (Acquired by JP Morgan Chase)
> *www.wamuproperties.com/*
> *Search Criteria: State, City, Zip, Type of Property, Bedrooms, Baths, Price*

Wells Fargo
> *www.pasreo.com/pasreo/public/propertySearch.do*
> *Search Criteria: State, City, Zip, County, Bedrooms, Bathrooms, Price*

Government Websites

Fannie Mae
> *http://reosearch.fanniemae.com/reosearch/*
> *Search Criteria: State, City, Zip, Price, Bedrooms, Baths*

Freddie Mac
> *www.homesteps.com/hm01_1featuresearch.htm*
> *Search Criteria: State, City, Zip, County, Price, Rooms, Bedrooms,*
> *Bathrooms*
> Freddie Mac Appraisal Form: *www.freddiemac.com/sell/forms/pdf/70.pdf*

GovernmentHousing.US
> *governmenthousing.us*
> *Search Criteria: State, County, City, Zip*

Homesales.gov
> *www.homesales.gov*
> *Search Criteria: State, Property Type*

U.S. Department of Housing and Urban Development
> *www.hud.gov/*
> *Search Criteria: State*

United States Marshal Services
> *www.treas.gov/auctions/treasury/rp/*
> *Sorted by State also includes other personal property*

U.S. Department of the Treasury
> *www.treas.gov/auctions/treasury/rp/*
> *Auction schedules for subject properties*
> **Internal Service:**
>> *www.treas.gov/auctions/irs/cat_Real7.htm*
>> *Properties are listed in order of State then City*

VA Homes for Sale
> *https://va.reotrans.com/index.cfm?*
> *Search Criteria: State, City, Zip, Bedrooms, Bathrooms, Price*

Asset Management Companies

Corporate Asset Management, LLC
> *www.camreo.com*
> *Search Criteria: Zip, Bedrooms, Baths, Property Type*

Grasha Real Estate
> *www.grasha.com/html/reo.lasso?-search=REO*

Keystone Asset Management
>   *www.keystonebest.com/*

LAMCO
>   *www.lendersreo.com/listings.aspx*
>   *Search Criteria: State, City, Price, Property Type*

Mortgage Lenders Network USA
>   *mlnusa.com*

OakTree Reo Asset Management
>   *www.gotooaktree.com/ASSET_20_MANAGEMENT.html*
>   *Search Criteria: City, County, Bedrooms, Baths, Property Type*

TREO
>   *www.treonet.com/*

TriMont Real Estate
>   *trimontrea.com/html/properties/properties_for_sale.asp*

Additional Finding Resources

Bid 4 Assets
>   *www.bid4assets.com/*
>   *Properties are listed by property type and when auction is closing*

Buy Bank Homes
>   *www.buybankhomes.com*
>   *Search Criteria: State, City, Zip, County*

Default Research Inc
>   *www.defaultresearch.com/*
>   *Listings available for purchase*

Foreclosurenet.net
>   *www.foreclosurenet.net/*
>   *Search Criteria: State, Zip*

Foreclosure.com
>   *www.foreclosure.com/*
>   *Search Criteria: State, Zip*

Foreclosures.com
>   *www.foreclosures.com/*
>   *Search Criteria: State, County, Zip*

Hudson and Marshall
>   *www.hudsonandmarshall.com/AuctionSchedule.aspx*
>   *Search Criteria: State, City, Zip*

Realtor.com
>   *www.realtor.com/FindHome/default.asp?mode=Map*

Realty Trac
www.realtytrac.com
Search Criteria: State, City, Zip

Sample Home Inspection Checklist

SITE ELEMENTS
- ☐ Ground Slope from Foundation
- ☐ Site Grading
- ☐ Irrigation Systems
- ☐ Retaining Walls
- ☐ Window Wells
- ☐ Patios
- ☐ Walkways
- ☐ Driveways

EXTERIOR ELEMENTS
- ☐ Entry Doors
- ☐ Windows
- ☐ Stairs/Stoops
- ☐ Porch(es)
- ☐ Siding (Brick, Vinyl, Aluminum, Stucco, Stone, Composite, Other)
- ☐ Deck(s)
- ☐ Railings
- ☐ Electrical Outlets

FOUNDATION AREA WATER PENETRATION
- ☐ Exterior Features/Water Intrusion Factors
- ☐ Interior Conditions/Signs of Water Intrusion

FOUNDATION/SUBSTRUCTURE
- ☐ Foundation Walls
- ☐ Basement Floor Slab

- ☐ Stairs
- ☐ Railings
- ☐ Floor Framing

ROOFING
- ☐ Roofing Shingles, Tiles, etc.
- ☐ Gutters
- ☐ Downspouts/Roof Drains
- ☐ Flashings
- ☐ Fascia/Soffits
- ☐ Chimneys
- ☐ Plumbing Stacks
- ☐ Ventilation Covers

GARAGE(S)
- ☐ Roofing
- ☐ Floor Slab
- ☐ Foundation
- ☐ Attic Ventilation
- ☐ Walls/Ceilings
- ☐ Siding
- ☐ Vehicle Doors
- ☐ Door Operators
- ☐ Electrical
- ☐ House/Service Doors

KITCHEN
- ☐ Plumbing/Sink
- ☐ Floor
- ☐ Walls/Ceiling
- ☐ Electrical/GFCI

☐ Oven
☐ Range
☐ Dishwasher
☐ Disposal
☐ Ventilator
☐ Cabinetry
☐ Countertops
☐ Refrigerator
☐ Interior Elements
☐ Ceilings
☐ Walls
☐ Floors
☐ Stairs
☐ Railings
☐ Windows
☐ Room Doors
☐ Slider/Patio Doors
☐ Smoke/CO Detectors
☐ Fireplaces

BATHROOM(S)
☐ Sink(s)
☐ Toilet
☐ Bathtub
☐ Shower
☐ Surround/Enclosure
☐ Flooring
☐ Walls/Ceiling
☐ Ventilator
☐ Electrical/GFCI

COOLING SYSTEM
☐ Outdoor Units
☐ Indoor Blower/Fan
☐ Condensation Provisions
☐ Thermostat(s)

ATTICS
☐ Roof Framing
☐ Roof Deck/Sheathing

☐ Ventilation Provisions
☐ Insulation

PLUMBING SYSTEM
☐ Water Supply Piping
☐ Water Flow at Fixtures
☐ Drain/Waste Piping
☐ Fixture Drainage
☐ Exterior Faucet(s)
☐ Gas Piping

ELECTRIC SYSTEM
☐ Service/Entrance Line
☐ Grounding Provisions
☐ Main Disconnect(s)
☐ Distribution Panel
☐ Devices
☐ Wiring/Conductors
☐ GFCI Test

HEATING SYSTEM
☐ Heating Unit
☐ Burner
☐ Fuel Line at Unit
☐ Combustion Air Provisions
☐ Vent Connector
☐ Blower
☐ Thermostat(s)

HOT WATER PIPING
☐ Water Heater
☐ Vent Connector
☐ Gas/Fuel Lines at Unit
☐ Safety Valve Provisions

200

Glossary of Terms

Abandonment: The voluntary renunciation of ownership or interest in real property by failure to use the property, coupled with the relinquishment of intent to vest ownership to any other person.

Abstract or Title Search: A summary of all recorded documents affecting a specific property. Used to determine the sufficiency and status of title for insurance of a title insurance policy.

Acceleration Clause: A provision in a contract that gives the lender the right to fully mature the time when the indebtedness becomes due, if the borrower defaults on the loan.

Acceptance: An offeree's written consent to enter into a contract and be bound by its terms.

Addendum: An addition or update to an existing contract.

Additional Principal Payment: Money paid by a borrower of more than the scheduled principal amount due, shortening the length of the loan.

Adjustable-Rate Mortgage (ARM): A mortgage with an interest rate that is periodically adjusted to more closely coincide with current rates.

Adjustment Date: The date on which an adjustable rate mortgage's interest rate is adjusted.

Adjustment Period: The amount of time between adjustment dates for an adjustable-rate mortgage.

Adverse Possession: A process of acquiring title to another's real property without compensation, by occupying the property for a statutory period of time.

Affordability Analysis: A detailed analysis of your income, liabilities, available funds, and the type of mortgage you plan to use, to determine your ability to afford the assumption of additional debt.

After Repair Value (ARV): An estimate of the value of a property after all repairs are completed.

Agent: One, who is authorized, either expressed or implied, to act on behalf of or represent another party.

Agreement of Sale: A legal document entered into between the buyer and seller for sale of real property. See "Real Estate Purchase Contract (REPC)."

Amortization: Literally "to kill off slowly," amortization is the process of repaying a mortgage loan through monthly installments of principal and interest where the annual interest amount adjusts as a multiple of the remaining principal balance.

Annual Percentage Rate (APR): The cost of borrowing money as an annual rate.

Annuity: A guaranteed minimum amount paid at regular intervals.

Appraisal: A professional analysis used to estimate the value of a property. This includes examples of sales of similar properties.

Appraised Value: An estimate of a property's fair market value, based on an appraiser's knowledge, experience, and analysis of the property.

Appraiser: A certified professional who is trained to conduct an analysis of real property, including the sales of comparable properties in order to develop an estimate of the subject property's value.

Appreciation: An increase in value over time.

As-Is Condition: A legal term used to disclaim implied warranties for a property being sold.

Asbestos: A toxic material that, prior to 1979, was used in housing insulation and fireproofing. Because some forms of asbestos have been linked to certain lung diseases, it is no longer used in new homes.

Assessed Value: Typically the value placed on property for the purpose of taxation.

Assessor: A public official who establishes the value of a property for taxation purposes.

Asset: Anything of monetary value that is owned by a person or company (i.e., real property, personal property, stocks, mutual funds).

Assignment: The transfer of rights and responsibilities from one party to another.

Assignor: The party that transfers rights and responsibilities to another.

Assumable Mortgage: A mortgage loan that is capable of being assumed by a different borrower. Typically, the original borrower remains liable unless released by the lender from the obligation. If the mortgage contains a due-on-sale clause, the loan may not be assumed without the lender's consent.

Assumption: The act of assuming another party's responsibility for paying an existing mortgage.

Assumption Fee: A fee a lender charges a buyer for processing new records when they assume the seller's existing mortgage.

Balance Sheet: A statement that lists a business's or individual's assets, liabilities, and net worth.

Balloon Loan: A type of mortgage that does not fully amortize over the term of the loan, leaving a larger lump sum payment due at maturity.

Bankrupt: The state of a party, having been declared financially unable to repay their debt when it is due.

Bankruptcy: A legal proceeding whereby a debtor can receive relief from payment of certain financial obligations. See "Chapter 7" and "Chapter 11."

Basis Point: A unit equal to 1/100 of one percentage point.

Before-Tax Income: Income before taxes are deducted. Also known as *Gross Income*.

Beneficiary: The party that receives benefits of fund or property under a deed, will, trust or insurance policy.

Bill of Sale: A legal document that transfers ownership of an asset from one party to another.

Binder: A temporary, binding agreement, used until a formal contract is established.

Biweekly Mortgage: A mortgage with payments due every two weeks (instead of monthly). This type of loan saves borrowers money by reducing the amount of interest accrued over the life of the loan.

Blanket Mortgage: A rare type of mortgage that covers more than one lot or parcel of real property.

Book Value: The value of a property, based on the purchase price of the property, plus the added value of improvements, minus depreciation.

Break-Even Point: The point at which expenses equal revenue; there is neither a net loss nor gain.

Borrower: A person who has applied and been approved to receive a loan and is then obligated to repay it according to the loan terms.

Breach of Contract: Failure to perform a contract, in whole or in part, without legal excuse.

Bridge Loan: A short-term loan that is to be paid back by a subsequent longer-term loan. Also known as a *Swing Loan* or *Interim Financing*.

Broker: A party that acts as an agent between providers and users of products or services, such as a mortgage broker or real estate broker.

Broker's Price Opinion (BPO): An estimate of a property's value by a real estate broker, based on the property's present condition, comparable sales, and market conditions for a quick sale.

Building Code: Local regulations that set forth the standards and requirements for the construction, maintenance and occupancy of real property.

Buydown: An arrangement whereby additional payments can be applied to the interest rate, that temporarily reduces the borrower's monthly payments.

Buyer's Market: A market that has more sellers than buyers. Low prices result from this excess of supply over demand. Also known as a *Soft Market*.

Buyer's Remorse: A nervousness or anxiety regarding a purchase that comes after the purchase has been made.

Call Option: A provision in a loan agreement that gives the lender the right to call the loan due and payable at the end of a specified period for whatever reason.

Cap: A limitation on how much the interest rate or payment may increase or decrease in an adjustable-rate mortgage.

Capacity: A borrowers ability to make payments on time. Based on income, income stability (job history and security), assets and savings, and the amount of income that is left over after regular housing costs, debt service and other obligations.

Capital Gains Tax: A tax assessed on profits realized from the sale of a capital asset, such as investment property and stock.

Capitalization: A mathematical process used by investors to derive the value of a property based using the rate of return on investments.

Capitalization Rate: The rate of return as it is estimated from the net income of an income property.

Carryback Financing: A type of seller financing whereby the seller agrees to carry a note for a specified portion of the contract price.

Carrying Costs: Costs incurred by an investor between purchasing a property and selling it. These costs may include debt service, taxes, utilities, and homeowner's dues.

Cash Flow: The amount of income a property produces after operating costs and loan payments have been made.

Cash for Keys: A proposition which a property owner would make with occupants of the property, in which the occupant is given cash in exchange for surrendering the keys and vacating the property.

Cash-on-Cash Return: A technique for calculating the return on an investment for which there is no secondary market. Equals the property's net income divided by the amount invested, expressed as a percentage.

Cash-out Refinance: A refinance transaction in which the borrower receives additional funds over and above the amount needed to repay the existing mortgage, closing costs, points, and any subordinate liens.

Certificate of Eligibility: A document issued by the U.S. Department of Veterans Affairs (VA) to verify the eligibility of a veteran for a VA-guaranteed loan.

Certificate of Occupancy: A document issued by the local government or building authority that states that a property meets all building codes and is suitable for occupancy.

Certificate of Reasonable Value (CRV): A document issued by the U.S. Department of Veterans Affairs (VA) that establishes the maximum value and loan amount for a VA mortgage.

Certificate of Title: In areas where attorneys examine abstracts or chains of title, a written opinion, executed by the examining attorney, stating that title is vested as stated in the abstract.

Chain of Title: The official record of all transfers of ownership, starting with the earliest existing document and ending with the most recent.

Change Orders: A change in the original construction plans ordered by the property owner or general contractor.

Chapter 7: A type of bankruptcy wherein the debtor is freed from their debts through the liquidation of virtually all of their assets.

Chapter 11: A type of bankruptcy wherein the debtor proposed a reorganization or repayment plan to satisfy creditors.

Clear Title: Ownership that is free of liens, defects, or other legal encumbrances.

Closing: The process of completing a financial transaction. For mortgage loans, the process of signing mortgage documents, disbursing funds, and, if applicable, transferring ownership of the property. Also known as *Settlement.*

Closing Costs: The expenses charged in connection with a mortgage loan or real estate transaction. Generally includes, but not limited to loan origination fees, title examination and insurance, survey, attorney's fee, and prepaid items, such as escrow deposits for taxes and insurance.

Closing Date: The date on which the sale of a property is to be finalized and a loan transaction completed.

Closing Statement: See "HUD-1 Settlement Statement."

Cloud on Title: Certain irregularities, possible claims, or encumbrances that appear on a title search, which, if valid, would negatively impact or impair the title.

Co-borrower: Any borrower other than the first borrower whose name appears on the application and mortgage note. Owns the property jointly with the first borrower and shares liability for the note.

Collateral: An asset that is pledged as security for a loan. The borrower risks losing the asset if the loan is not repaid according to the terms of the loan agreement. In the case of a mortgage, the collateral would be the house and real property.

Collateralized Mortgage Obligations (CMO): A type of security that is backed by a pool of mortgages.

Commission: Compensation charged for services performed, usually based on a percentage of the price of the items sold (such as the fee a real estate agent earns on the sale of a property).

Commitment Letter: A binding offer from your lender that includes the amount of the mortgage, the interest rate, and repayment terms.

Comparable Sales: The recent selling prices of similar properties, which are used as a comparison in determining the current value of a property that is being appraised. Also called *Comps* or *Comparables*.

Compound Interest: Interest that is calculated on the principal balance of a loan as well as accrued interest.

Concessions: Cash or other equivalent that is given up or agreed upon in negotiating the sale of real property. For example, the sellers may agree to help pay a portion of the closing costs, offer an allowance replace the carpet, or put funds in an escrow account rather than warranty a portion of the home.

Condemnation: A government agency's act of taking private property for public use, such as for a street or a storm drain. Also known as *Eminent Domain*.

Consensual Liens: Liens imposed by a contract between the creditor and the debtor. These liens include: mortgages, car loans, security interests, and chattel mortgages.

Construction Loan: A loan for financing the cost of construction or improvements to a property; the lender disburses payments to the builder at periodic intervals during construction.

Constructive Notice: Notice imparted by the public records of the county when documents entitled to recording are recorded.

Consumer Price Index (CPI): A measurement of inflation, relating to the change in the cost of a fixed basket of goods and services, including housing, electricity, food and transportation. Also called the *Cost-of-Living Index.*

Contingency: A condition that must be met before a contract is legally binding. For example, home purchasers often include a home inspection contingency; the sales contract is not binding unless and until the purchaser has the home inspected.

Contract: A binding agreement between two or more parties to perform or not to perform a some specific act(s) in exchange for lawful consideration.

Conventional Mortgage: A mortgage loan that is not insured or guaranteed by the Federal government or one of its agencies, such as the Federal Housing Administration (FHA), the U.S. Department of Veterans Affairs (VA), or the Rural Housing Service (RHS).

Convertible Adjustable-Rate Mortgage: An adjustable-rate mortgage (ARM) that allows the borrower to convert the loan to a fixed-rate mortgage under specified conditions.

Conveyance: An instrument in writing, such as a deed or trust deed, used to transfer title to property from one party to another.

Cooperative (Co-op) Project: A project in which a corporation holds title to property and sells shares to individual buyers, who then receive a proprietary lease as their title.

Co-Signer: A second party that also signs a promissory note, thereby taking responsibility for the debt in the event that the first party does not.

Cost of Capital: The opportunity cost of an investment; that is, the rate of return that could have otherwise been earned at the same risk level as the investment that was selected.

Counter-Offer: An offer made in response to a previous offer.

Covenants, Conditions and Restrictions: Refers to a written recorded declaration of certain covenants, conditions, restrictions, rules or regulations established by a subdivider or other landowner to create uniformity of buildings and use. Also known as *CC & R's* or *Private Zoning.*

Credit: The ability of a person to borrow money, or buy goods by paying over time. Credit is extended based on a lender's opinion of the person's financial situation and reliability, among other factors.

Credit Bureau: A company that gathers information on consumers who use credit. These companies sell that information to lenders and other businesses in the form of a credit report.

Credit History: Information in the files of a credit bureau, primarily comprised of a list of individual consumer debts and a record of whether or not these debts were paid back on time or as agreed.

Credit Life Insurance: A type of insurance that pays off a specific amount of debt or a specified credit account if the borrower dies while the policy is in force.

Credit Rating: The degree of creditworthiness of an individual, based on his credit history and current financial condition.

Credit Report: Information provided by a credit bureau that allows a lender or other business to examine your use of credit. It provides information on money that you've borrowed and your payment history.

Credit Score: A numerical value that represents a borrower's credit risk based on an evaluation of the information in the individual's credit history.

Creditor: A person or organization, which extends credit to others.

Days on Market (DOM): The number of days a listing is active in a multiple listing service before an offer has been accepted by the seller but the transaction is not yet closed.

Debt: Money owed from one party to another.

Debt Discharge Income: If you owe a debt to someone else and they cancel or forgive that debt, the canceled amount may be taxable as income. However, the Mortgage Debt Relief Act of 2007 generally allows taxpayers to exclude income from the discharge of debt on their principal residence.

Debt Service: The amount of money required over a given period for the repayment of interest and principal on a debt.

Debt-to-Income Ratio: A mathematical measure of creditworthiness. Calculates how much of a person's monthly gross income is spent paying debts by dividing monthly debt owed by monthly income.

Debtor: One who owes a debt to another.

Deed: A legal document that conveys ownership.

Deed-in-Lieu of Foreclosure: A situation in which a deed is given to the lender in order to satisfy the mortgage debt and avoid foreclosure.

Deed of Trust or Trust Deed: A written document by which the title to land is conveyed as security for the repayment of a loan or other obligation.

Default: Failure to fulfill a legal obligation. A default includes failure to pay on a financial obligation, but also may be a failure to perform some action or service that is non-monetary.

Deficiency Judgment: A judgment lien against a debtor whose foreclosure sale did not produce sufficient funds to pay the mortgage in full.

Deleveraging: An attempt to decrease financial leverage, to return to price and value equilibrium. Also known as *Reset*.

Delinquency: Failure to make a required payment when it is due.

Depreciation: A decline in the value due to changing market conditions.

Disclosure: A written statement, revealing all the known facts that may affect the decision of a potential buyer or tenant.

Discount Points: A fee paid by the borrower at closing to reduce the interest rate. A point equals one percent of the loan amount.

Discount Rate: A figure used to translate future cash flows to Net Present Value. Also known as *Capitalization Rate*.

Diversification: An investment strategy designed to reduce risk by combing a variety of investments which are unlikely to all move in the same direction.

Down Payment: A portion of the price of a home, usually between 3-20 percent, not borrowed and paid up-front in cash.

Due Diligence: The process of investigation, performed by investors, into the details of a potential investment, to confirm that the property is as represented and is not subject to undisclosed problems.

Due on Sale Clause: A contractual term that allows the lender to demand repayment in full of the outstanding balance if the property securing the mortgage is sold.

Earnest Money: Consideration given by a buyer to a seller to bind a contract. In a real estate purchase contract (REPC), the earnest money deposit may or may not be fully refundable, based on the terms and contingencies of the contract.

Easement: A right or interest in the use of the land of another party, which entitles the holder to some use, privilege or benefit.

Effective Age: An appraiser's estimate of the physical condition of a building. The actual age of a building may be shorter or longer than its effective age.

Eminent Domain: See "Condemnation."

Encroachment: Any improvement that overlaps onto the property of an adjoining owner.

Encumbrance: Any lien or limitation on the ownership of the land that interferes with using it or transferring ownership. For example: mortgages, deeds of trust, mechanics' liens, taxes, CC & R's, easements, etc.).

Equal Credit Opportunity Act (ECOA): A Federal law that requires lenders to make credit equally available without regard to the applicant's race, color, religion, national origin, age, sex, or marital status.

Equity: The value of a property above the total amount of the liens against the property. For example, if you owe $100,000 on your house but it is worth $130,000, you have $30,000 of equity.

Errors and Omissions Insurance (E&O): A type of liability insurance that protects insured professionals from damages caused by their errors or oversight.

Escrow: An item of value, money, or documents deposited with a third party (escrow agent) to be delivered upon the fulfillment of a condition.

Escrow Account: An account held in the borrower's name to pay taxes, insurance premiums, or other charges when they are due. Also known as an *Impound* or *Reserve* account.

Eviction: The legal act of removing someone from real property.

Exclusive Agency Listing: A written agreement under which a real estate professional is given the exclusive right to sell a property for the property owner, but may be paid a reduced or no commission when the property is sold if, for example, the property owner rather than the agent finds a buyer.

Exclusive Right-to-Sell Listing: The traditional type of listing agreement under which the property owner appoints a real estate professional the exclusive agent to sell the property on the owner's stated terms, and agrees to pay the listing broker a commission when the property is sold, regardless of whether the buyer is found by the broker, the owner or another broker.

Exit Strategy: The way in which an investor closes out all or part of an investment.

Fair Credit Reporting Act (FCRA): A consumer protection law that governs the processes credit bureaus must follow.

Fair Housing Act: Federal legislation that prohibits discrimination in all facets of the home buying process on the basis of race, color, national origin, religion, sex, familial status, or disability.

Fair Market Value: The price at which property would be transferred between willing (but not desperate) buyers and sellers, with full disclosure.

Fannie Mae: A public company that operates under a Federal charter as the nation's largest source of financing for home mortgages. The company buys mortgage loans from lending institutions and resells them as securities on the secondary mortgage market.

Feasibility: The likelihood that an investment will fulfill the objectives of a particular party, in terms of costs and revenue.

Federal Housing Administration (FHA): A government agency within the U.S. Department of Housing and Urban Development (HUD) that insures mortgages and loans made by private lenders.

Fee Simple: The highest form of ownership in real property. An estate under which the owner is entitled to unrestricted use or transfer of the property, save only government limitations (i.e., zoning).

FHA-Insured Loan: A loan that is insured by the Federal Housing Administration (FHA) of the U.S. Department of Housing and Urban Development (HUD).

First Mortgage: A mortgage that is the primary lien against a property.

First-Time Home Buyer: A person that has not had an ownership interest in a primary residence during the three-year period preceding the purchase of real property.

Fixed-Period Adjustable-Rate Mortgage: An adjustable-rate mortgage (ARM) that offers a fixed rate for an initial period and then adjusts at set periods for the remainder of the term. Also known as a *Hybrid Loan*.

Fixed-Rate Mortgage: A mortgage with an interest rate that does not change during the entire term of the loan.

Flood Certification: The process of determining whether or not a property is located in a designated flood zone.

Flood Insurance: Insurance that compensates for physical property damage resulting from flooding. Required for properties located in Federally designated flood zones.

For Sale By Owner (FSBO): The process of selling real estate without the marketing or representation of a real estate professional.

Forbearance: A loss mitigation option where the lender arranges a revised repayment plan for the borrower that may include a temporary reduction or suspension of monthly loan payments. Also known as a *Workout Agreement*.

Foreclosure: A legal action that ends all ownership rights in a home when the home buyer fails to make the mortgage payments or is otherwise in default under the terms of the mortgage.

Freddie Mac: A government agency that purchases conventional first and second mortgages that are guaranteed by the FHA or VA from members of the Federal Reserve System and the Federal Home Loan Bank System, and then sells them to investors in order to generate funds for lenders to grant new loans.

Fully Amortized Mortgage: A mortgage in which the monthly payments are designed to pay off and retire the loan at the end of the mortgage term.

General Contractor: A person who performs or oversees the construction or development of a home improvement or construction project and handles various aspects such as scheduling workers and ordering supplies.

Ginnie Mae: See "Government National Mortgage Association."

Good Faith Estimate: A form required by the Real Estate Settlement Procedures Act (RESPA) that discloses an estimate of the amount or range of charges, for specific settlement services the borrower is likely to incur in connection with the mortgage transaction.

Government Mortgage: A mortgage loan that is insured or guaranteed by a Federal government entity such as the Federal Housing Administration (FHA), the U.S. Department of Veterans Affairs (VA), or the Rural Housing Service (RHS).

Government National Mortgage Association: A government-owned corporation within the U.S. Department of Housing and Urban Development (HUD) that guarantees securities backed by mortgages that are insured or guaranteed by other government agencies. Also known as *Ginnie Mae*.

Grace Period: An additional period of time allowed beyond the due date to make a payment without penalty.

Gross Income: See "Before-Tax Income."

Gross Rent Multiplier (GRM): A formula yielding a generic rule of thumb for comparing income properties. GRM is arrived at by dividing the sales price by the annual income from rents. GRM is not considered a thorough vetting of an investment's potential.

Growing-Equity Mortgage (GEM): A fixed-rate mortgage that bears scheduled increases in the monthly payment with the additional funds credited against the loan balance and the reduction of the loan term.

Guaranteed Maximum Price (GMP): A contract for which a contractor agrees to provide a specific scope of work for a specified maximum price. The contractor is responsible for any cost overruns, unless the GMP has been increased via formal change order.

Hard Cost: In construction or rehabilitation, these are the costs that are directly associated with improvements to the property. Compare with Soft Costs.

Hazard Insurance: See "Homeowners Insurance."

Highest and Best Use: Real property appraisers consider whether or not a property is being put to the use that has the potential to reasonably produce the most value. In order for uses to be considered, they cannot be impossible, illegal, or financially improbable.

Home Equity Conversion Mortgage (HECM): A special type of mortgage developed and insured by the Federal Housing Administration (FHA) that enables older homeowners to convert the equity they have in their homes into cash, using a variety of payment options to address their specific financial needs. Sometimes called a "reverse mortgage."

Home Equity Line of Credit (HELOC): A line of credit or revolving loan secured by the equity over and above other liens on the property. Borrowers under this type of loan can obtain multiple advances of the loan proceeds, up to the total amount of the loan.

Home Inspection: A professional inspection of a home to determine the condition of the property. The inspection should include an evaluation of the plumbing, heating and cooling systems, roof, wiring, foundation and pest infestation.

Homeowners' Association (HOA): HOAs are typically non-profit corporations founded by a builder or developer of a community and then transferred to the homeowners who live there. They often have responsibility over common facilities and have the right to place a lien on properties whose owners fail to pay dues, assessments or maintenance fees according to the CC&R's.

Homeowners Insurance: Insurance against disasters like flood and fire, as well as liabilities, such as an injury to a visitor to your home. These policies can even protect your personal property, such as your furniture, clothes or appliances. Homeowners insurance is typically required by lenders on the collateral property in order to protect the lender's interests.

Homeowner's Warranty: Insurance offered by a seller that covers a home for a specified period for the cost of certain repairs to fixtures and systems which may have been defective or for some reason experienced a shortened useful life.

Housing Expense Ratio: The percentage of a borrower's gross monthly income that goes toward paying for housing expenses.

HUD (Housing and Urban Development): The U.S. Department of Housing and Urban Development is the government office responsible for administering housing programs.

HUD-1 Settlement Statement: As required by RESPA, a document that lists all closing and financing costs on a consumer mortgage transaction. It provides the sales price and down payment, as well as the total settlement costs required from the buyer and seller.

Hurdle Rate: The required rate of return when using a discounted cash flow analysis. Rates of return above the hurdle rate indicate that an investment makes sense—below it, however, the investment does not. Often, this is a function of the cost of capital, plus or minus a risk premium to reflect the project's specific risk characteristics. Also called *Required Rate of Return.*

Hybrid Loan: An adjustable-rate mortgage (ARM) that offers a fixed rate for an initial period, typically three to ten years, and then adjusts every six months, annually, or at another specified period, based on an index (such as the prime rate) for the remainder of the term.

Improvements: Permanent additions that can legally be considered part of a piece of real property.

Income Property: Typically rental property. See "Investment Property."

Inflation: Increase in prices typically expressed as a higher cost of goods and services. Inflation is caused by growth in money supply which exceeds growth in the Gross Domestic Product (GDP).

Initial Interest Rate: The original interest rate for an adjustable-rate mortgage (ARM). Sometimes known as the "start rate."

Interest Accrual Rate: The percentage rate at which interest accumulates or accrues on a mortgage loan.

Interest-Only Loan: Loans in which the initial mortgage payments consist of only interest, rather than both principal and interest. This type of mortgage was popular in the run-up to the sub-prime mortgage crisis.

Interest Rate: This is the cost to the borrower for using the lender's money. Interest rates typically represent annual percentages against the original principal amount.

Interest Rate Cap: In an adjustable rate mortgage (ARM), the limitation on the amount the interest rate can change per adjustment or over the lifetime of the loan.

Interest Rate Ceiling: In an adjustable rate mortgage (ARM), the maximum interest rate, as specified in the mortgage note.

Interest Rate Floor: In an adjustable rate mortgage (ARM), this represents the minimum interest rate, as specified in the mortgage note.

Internal Rate of Return (IRR): A tool for comparative analysis between two investment alternatives. IRR tells us what rate of return is sufficient to make the NPV of future cash flows plus the final market value of an investment or business opportunity zero out or break even.

Intrinsic Value: The actual value of a property, company, or security, when all salient facts are considered as opposed to merely its market price or book value.

Investment Property: A property purchased with the intent that it generate an ROI, either from a subsequent sale or from the generation of rental income or tax benefits rather than to serve as the borrower's primary residence. Contrast with Second Home.

Joint Tenancy: A form of co-ownership that gives each tenant equal interest and equal rights in the property, including the right of survivorship.

Judgment Lien: A lien resulting from a court-ordered judgment against debtor with an interest in the property, and for whom the court has decided that the property represents a method for discharge or partial discharge of the debt.

Judicial Foreclosure: Foreclosures in states that require that they be processed through the court system.

Jumbo Loan: Loans on expensive homes. In other words, homes with original principal balances in excess of the mortgage amount eligible for purchase by Fannie Mae or Freddie Mac (currently this ranges from $417,000 to $938,250 depending on your area).

Junior Mortgage: A mortgage loan that is subordinate to the first mortgage or first-lien mortgage loan, such as a second or third mortgage.

Late Charge: A fee imposed by the lender if a borrower makes a late payment.

Late Payment: Payment made by the borrower to the lender after the required date as specified in the payment schedule.

Lease: An agreement between the owner of real property (the lessor), in which the right of possession is granted to another (the lessee), for a specified period of time (term) and for a specified consideration (rent).

Lease Option: A lease which also grants the lessee an option to purchase under certain terms and conditions. Typically, part of each rental payment is put aside for the purpose of accumulating funds to pay the down payment and closing costs.

Legal Description: A description of land recognized by law, based on government surveys, delineating the exact boundaries of an entire parcel of land. It should so discretely identify a parcel of land so that it cannot be confused with any other.

Lender: Any person or entity advancing funds which are to be repaid. A general term encompassing all mortgagees, and beneficiaries under mortgage agreements and deeds of trust.

Letter of Intent (LOI): A document delivered to the seller indicating that a buyer is interested in the property listed for sale at a specified purchase price and under specified conditions. A letter of intent is not a contract and is not binding on either party.

Leverage: Borrowing money to supplement existing funds for investment in order to magnify or enhance the scope of the potential positive or negative outcome.

Liabilities: Debts and other financial obligations.

Liability Insurance: Insurance purchased to protect property owners against claims of negligence, personal injury or property damage to another party.

LIBOR (London InterBank Offered Rate): An index used to determine interest rate changes for certain adjustable-rate mortgage (ARM) plans, based on the average interest rate at which international banks lend to or borrow funds.

Lien: An encumbrance on the title to real property as collateral or security for payment of a debt. Mortgages and deeds of trust are liens which include foreclosure rights. Foreclosure is the process by which the collateral is repossessed and disposed of to pay the outstanding debt.

Lifetime Cap: For an adjustable-rate mortgage (ARM), a limit on the amount that the interest rate or monthly payment can increase or decrease over the life of the loan.

Liquid Asset: A cash asset or an asset that is easily converted into cash.

Lis Pendens: A notice or a claim of interest in the property and that the claim of interest is the subject of a lawsuit.

Loan Fraud: Purposely giving incorrect information on a loan application in order to better qualify for a loan. Fraud carries the risk of serious civil liability and/or criminal penalties.

Loan Origination: The manner in which new loans are generated and made, which may include taking a loan application, processing and underwriting the application, and closing the loan.

Loan Origination Fees: Fees paid to your mortgage lender or broker for processing the mortgage application and originating the loan. This fee is usually in the form of points. One point equals one percent of the mortgage amount.

Loan-To-Value (LTV) Ratio: The relationship between the loan amount and the value of the property (the lower of appraised value or sales price), expressed as a percentage of the property's value. For example, a $100,000 home with an $80,000 mortgage has an LTV of 80 percent.

Lock-In Rate: A written agreement guaranteeing a specific mortgage interest rate for a certain amount of time.

Loss Mitigation: Lender's terminology for any process enacted to prevent borrowers from going into foreclosure. This department often handles loan modifications and short sale offers.

Manufactured Housing: Homes that are factory-built in accordance with specific Federal building codes administered by the U.S. Department of Housing and Urban Development (HUD) and then assembled on-site. Homes that are permanently affixed to a foundation are generally classified as real property under applicable state law, and qualify for traditional mortgage financing. However, homes not permanently affixed to a foundation are typically classified as personal property, and require financing via a retail installment sales agreement.

Market Value: The current value of a property based on what buyers in the current local market would pay. An appraisal is sometimes used by lenders to determine market value.

Marketable Title: Title to real property that is free from defects, clouds and encumbrances which would restrict the issuance of title insurance, and free from any reasonable risk of litigation.

Maturity Date: The date, as stated in the note, on which a mortgage loan is scheduled to be completely paid in full.

Mechanic's Lien: A lien created by statute when a contractor or sub-contractor files it after performing work, which becomes an improvement and a permanent part of real property. These liens exist for the purpose of securing priority of payment.

Merged Credit Report: A credit report issued by a credit reporting company that combines information from two or three major credit bureaus.

Mezzanine Financing: Hybrid financing between traditional debt and equity. Investors start out as debt holders, but are given the right to convert to equity shareholders if the loan is not repaid according to the terms of the financing. Rates of return are generally fairly aggressive and these debts are typically junior to banks or venture capitalists.

Modification: Any change to the terms of a mortgage loan, including changes to the interest rate, loan balance, or loan term, specifically those made in an effort to avoid foreclosure.

Modified Internal Rate of Return (MIRR): A modification of the internal rate of return (IRR). Instead of assuming that a project's cash flows are to be invested at the IRR, MIRR assumes that the cash flows are instead invested at the firm's cost of capital (often its weighted average cost of capital or WACC). It is designed to better take into account the compounding of reinvested cash flows.

Mortgage: A loan secured by real property as collateral. In practice, this term may refer to a true mortgage or to a deed of trust (see "Deed of Trust"). It also may be used to indicate the amount of money borrowed, with interest, to purchase a property. The amount of a mortgage often is the purchase price of the home less any down payment.

Mortgage Broker: An individual or firm that brokers loans between borrowers and lenders. A mortgage broker typically takes loan applications and may process and close loans. Mortgage brokerages typically do not service their loans long-term.

Mortgage Insurance (MI): Insurance paid by borrowers which protects lenders against losses caused by a borrower's mortgage loan default. MI typically is required if the borrower's down payment is less than 20 percent of the purchase price. (Some lenders have now bumped this to 22 percent in response to the current credit crunch.)

Mortgage Insurance Premium (MIP): Borrowers pay this amount for mortgage insurance, either to a government agency such as the Federal Housing Administration (FHA) or to a private mortgage insurance (PMI) company.

Mortgage Interest Deduction: In the U.S. interest paid on mortgage loans for first and second homes is tax deductible for income tax purposes.

Mortgage Life and Disability Insurance: A type of insurance that will payoff a mortgage upon the borrower's death as long as the loan is outstanding.

Mortgagee: The lender. This is the party lending the money and receiving the mortgage.

Mortgagor: The borrower. Technically, this is the party who gives the mortgage.

Multiple Listing Service (MLS): A database of property listing and sale information. Access to the MLS is one of the advantages of hiring a Realtor. Seller's gain the exposure as their listing is available for any buyer's agent to see who is a member. Likewise buyers get a broader list of homes from which to choose. The MLS for an area is usually operated by the local, private real estate association as a joint venture among its members designed to foster real estate brokerage services.

Negative Amortization: An increase in the principal balance of a loan as unpaid interest is added to the loan balance; this occurs when payments are insufficient to cover the interest due, such as when the interest rate increases due to an adjustable rate mortgage (ARM).

Net Operating Income (NOI): In income property financials, NOI represents operating expenses subtracted from gross income. NOI is used to calculate the cap rate.

Net Present Value (NPV): A calculation used to determine the present value of an investment's future net cash flows minus the initial investment. A positive NPV indicates that the investment should be made barring more attractive alternatives.

Net Worth: The sum of the balance sheet—assets less liabilities. This applies to companies as well as individuals.

Non-Assumption Clause: A mortgage contract term prohibiting another borrower from assuming the loan without first obtaining approval from the lender.

Non-Consensual Liens: Also called statutory or involuntary liens, these liens arise by statute or by the operation of laws enacted to protect creditors. These liens include: tax liens, imposed to secure payment of a tax; mechanic's liens, which secure payment for work done on property or land; and judgment liens, imposed to secure payment of a judgment.

Non-Judicial Foreclosure: Foreclosure governed by contract and private parties in accord with state law, without the involvement of the courts.

Non-Liquid Asset: An asset that cannot easily be converted into cash.

Non-Performing Loan: A loan in default.

Note: A unilateral agreement containing an express and absolute promise of the signer to pay to a named person, or order, or bearer, a definite sum of money at a specified date or on demand. Usually provides for interest and, concerning real property, is secured by a mortgage or trust deed.

Note Rate: The interest rate stated on a mortgage note, or other loan agreement.

Notice of Default (NOD): The recorded notice that a borrower is in default, has failed to live up to the terms of the mortgage contract, and that the lender intends to enforce its right to foreclose.

Notice of Sale: The recorded notice (required to be posted by lenders) notifying the public that a property is to be sold at a foreclosure auction.

Offer: Often submitted as a REPC, offers tell sellers the price and terms under which a buyer is willing to purchase the property. When bidding on REOs, offers are a factor of your maximum bid.

Open House: Times when a property on the market for sale is open for viewing by anyone without a prior appointment. Representation by a real estate agent is not required to attend an open house.

Original Cost: The seller's original purchase price for the property. This may not be the original selling price of the home, when new, but may be a significant reference point when it comes to negotiating with the seller.

Original Principal Balance: The total principal amount of a mortgage before any payments are made.

Origination Fee: Typically stated in points (see "Points") origination fees are paid to a lender or mortgage broker as part of the administrative costs of processing a loan application.

Parcel: Land within a specific legal description.

Partial Payment: Payments less than the full amount required by the mortgage agreement.

Partnership: Two or more people bound together in a business venture by contract. The contract establishes the proportionate responsibility to bear costs and share in profits.

Payment Cap: The extent to which payments can increase on an adjustable-rate mortgage (ARM), or other variable rate loan, during any adjustment period.

Payment Change Date: The date on which a new monthly payment amount takes effect, for example, on an adjustable rate mortgage (ARM) loan.

Per-Diem Interest: When closing occurs mid-month, interest is paid on the partial month on a daily pro rata or Per Diem basis. In other words if the property belonged to the seller for 15 days in the month of closing, the seller is responsible to pay the lender for 15 days worth of interest at closing.

Personal Property (movable): As opposed to real property, personal property includes items not designated by law as real property such as money, goods, evidences of debt, rights of action, chattels furniture, automobiles, etc.

PITI: An acronym for principle, interest, taxes, and insurance, the four primary components of a monthly mortgage payment.

Planned Unit Development (PUD): A subdivision with prescribed land uses according to a unified master plan. Sometimes PUDs incorporate common areas governed by an HOA.

Plat: Scale maps of property showing boundaries and divisions. Often prepared by a surveyor and of particular interest if parcels of property are being combined or subdivided.

Point: One percentage point of the mortgage loan amount. For example, if a loan is made for $100,000, one point equals $1,000.

Power of Attorney: A document granting legal authority for one person to act in behalf of another. For instance, a family member may be granted power of attorney in order to complete the sale of real property on behalf of the owner.

Pre-Approval: Also, pre-qualification. A preliminary estimate of a borrower's ability to qualify and obtain a mortgage loan for a specified amount in anticipation of purchasing a specific property. Typically prospective borrowers go through much of the process of obtaining a loan, in order for the lender to issue a pre-approval.

Pre-Foreclosure Sale: Sales during the pre-foreclosure period, which includes any sale prior to the public foreclosure auction.

Predatory Lending: Unethical lending practices like encouraging borrowers to refinance their mortgage and extract the equity purely for the purpose of making money on loan fees, unnecessary insurance, etc. This is particularly abusive when borrowers are manipulated by mortgage brokers through fear and dishonest representations and when the borrowers are knowingly not financially able to service the new level of indebtedness.

Prepayment: Payments reducing the principal balance of a loan ahead of the payment schedule.

Prepayment Penalty: A fee charged to borrowers for paying off the mortgage ahead of schedule, or making substantial reduction in the remaining principal balance on the loan.

Principal: The amount of the original loan which has not yet been repaid. Interest represents the amount over and above the principal paid by borrowers for the privilege of borrowing the principal amount. The principal balance (sometimes called the outstanding or unpaid principal balance) is the amount owed on the loan minus what has been repaid.

Priority: The established seniority of the various liens and encumbrances affecting the title to a piece of real property. The recording date often determines the priority and position of various liens on a property.

Private Mortgage Insurance (PMI): See "Mortgage Insurance."

Promissory Note: A written promise to repay a specified amount over a specified period of time.

Property Tax: Taxes assessed to owners of real property. Property taxes are always senior in position to private liens.

Public Records: Those documents legally recorded in the recorder's office, such as notices, liens, transfers, etc.

Purchase Agreement: See "Real Estate Purchase Contract (REPC)."

Quiet Title: Established by a lawsuit, the court with jurisdiction over a property may put down any claims of interest which show up as clouds or claims against the title of that property by issuing an action or decree to quiet the title.

Quitclaim Deed: An instrument often used to gift real property from one party to another. The person relinquishing interest in the property vacates any claim to it and assigns the claim of interest they may have had to another party. There is no insurance or warranty that the person relinquishing a claim of interest actually has a valid claim of interest.

Radon: A naturally occurring radioactive toxic gas produced by the decay of uranium. It is colorless and odorless and can enter buildings from the rocks and soil beneath and around them. Radon can cause lung cancer and other illnesses.

Rate Cap: The extent to which the interest rate on an adjustable-rate mortgage (ARM) can increase during any single adjustment period.

Rate Lock: An agreement in which an interest rate is locked in or guaranteed for a specified period of time prior to closing. See "Lock-in Rate."

Rating: A measure of the riskiness of a security as determined by a rating agency.

Rating Agencies: Also a credit rating agency (CRA). Rating agencies are companies who issue ratings on securities. Good ratings indicate low risk and high likelihood of increasing value based on the opinion of the rating agency. Conversely, low ratings indicate high risk and low likelihood of increasing value.

Real Estate Owned (REO): Properties which fail to sell at a public foreclosure auction return to the ownership of the lender as REO or bank-owned property.

Real Estate Purchase Contract (REPC): The legal contract between a buyer and a seller relating to the purchase of real property. The REPC terms govern the responsibilities and conditions of each party as well as detailing the essential terms of the transaction like the names of the buyer and seller, the property address, the purchase price, etc.

Real Estate Settlement Procedures Act (RESPA): A Federal law that requires lenders to provide home mortgage borrowers with information about transaction-related costs prior to settlement, as well as information during the life of the loan regarding servicing and escrow accounts. RESPA also prohibits kickbacks and unearned fees in the mortgage loan business.

Real Property (immovable): Land and permanently affixed improvements such as buildings, roads, or utility structures. Real property is associated with property rights such as ownership, mineral rights, easements, rights of way, etc.

Realtor: A real estate professional who is also a member of the National Association of Realtors.

Recorder: Synonymous with a Register of Deeds or County Clerk, this is the public official responsible for keeping the public records relating to real property transactions in the area. This is typically a county-level position.

Recording: The act of entering documents into the public record such as notices, liens, transfers, purchases, etc. The recording process is governed by the laws and statutes of the specific jurisdiction.

Redemption Period: The period after a foreclosure auction during which a borrower may still reclaim the property by paying off the lender's lien.

Refinance: Obtaining a mortgage loan which pays off and replaces a prior mortgage on a property.

Reinstatement Period: Time between the acceleration of a mortgage in default and just prior to the public foreclosure auction in which the borrower's ownership may be reinstated and foreclosure averted by either paying off all liens on the property, or bringing all loans and lender fees current.

Repayment Plan: A workout between the lender and the borrower allowing the borrower to bring missed payments current by making payments according to a fixed schedule.

Replacement Cost: The method of valuing real property based on the actual cost to rebuild the property if it were destroyed.

Required Rate of Return: See "Hurdle Rate."

Rescission: The cancellation or annulment of a transaction or contract according to specific terms. Many contracts and state laws provide for a right of rescission as a method of protecting borrowers who may have been coerced, victims of high-pressure sales tactics, or who simply experience buyer's remorse.

Return of Capital: Return of the original capital outlay in an investment. Return of capital is not considered income or a return on investment (ROI).

Return on Investment: The returns an investment produces over and above the return of capital.

Reverse Mortgage: A type of mortgage targeted at seniors in which the mortgage debt increases over time, and borrowers withdraw equity they have built up over time.

Right of First Refusal: A provision granting a specified party the right to purchase or lease a property before that property is made available for purchase or lease by others.

Sale-Leaseback: When the owner of a property sells it to a buyer, but continues to occupy the property under a lease agreement. The seller becomes the tenant; the buyer becomes the landlord.

Second Mortgage: A mortgage subordinate and subsequent to a first mortgage. The new mortgage is in *second* position relative to the first.

Secondary Market: If mortgage brokers are the retailers, the secondary mortgage market are the wholesalers. The secondary market typically holds mortgages throughout their term and dictates underwriting requirements that influence the primary mortgage market. Fannie Mae and Freddie Mac are considered major players in the secondary mortgage market.

Secured Loan: When a loan is attached to collateral which may be sold to discharge the debt, it is said to be *secured*. Mortgages are loans secured by real property, but other loans, like auto loans, which are tied to collateral are also secured loans.

Securities and Exchange Commission (SEC): Created by the Securities and Exchange Act of 1934 in response to the stock market crashes precipitating the Great Depression, the SEC is the regulatory body in the U.S. responsible for regulating the secondary trading or exchange of securities and enforcing securities laws.

Securitization: The act of financial structuring (typically with debt and/or equity) of financial entities so that securities can be issued and purchased by investors.

Security: Financial instruments such as stocks or bonds which represent ownership in a government or financial entity and which may be purchased and sold according to the rules of the governing regulatory body over securities exchanges (the SEC in the U.S.)

Seller Carry-Back: Typically used when a borrower cannot secure financing for the total purchase price of a property, the seller acts as the lender of a second mortgage which the buyer pays in addition to any traditional financing.

Seller Financing: A purchase in which the seller acts as a lender for all or part of the purchase price, typically because the buyer does not qualify for traditional financing.

Seller's Market: In a seller's market prices and negotiated terms which sweeten the deal for sellers occur because buyers are more plentiful than sellers creating demand greater than the supply.

Settlement: Another term for *Closing*. Settlement is where the purchase of real property is completed including all signatures, mortgage documents if any, title work, escrow and funding details and legal transfer of ownership.

Settlement Statement: See "HUD-1 Settlement Statement."

Short Sale / Short Payoff Sale: When a property will not sell for an amount sufficient to pay off the balance owed to any lenders, the lender(s) may agree to take less than the balance owed under the rationale that this would be preferable to the property going into foreclosure.

Soft Cost: In lending and construction, soft costs are typically those relating to professional services rather than the purchase price, loan amount, or cost of construction. Soft costs may include expenses relating to architects, attorneys, Realtors, engineers, inspectors, and finance professionals.

Special Assessment: Tax districts and HOAs may incur costs for which their budgets are inadequate, but which constitute emergency or essential services. The costs of these services are levied against all the members or constituents or the relevant body in a Special Assessment.

Squatter: A person settling upon an unoccupied property without any legal right. See "Adverse Possession."

Staging: Preparing the presentation of a property so that it will have the greatest appeal to potential buyers.

Subcontractor: In contrast with general contractors, subcontractors are typically licensed only to perform contract work of a specific type like plumbing, framing or electrical work.

Subdivision: A parcel of land, which has been legally subdivided into individual building lots. These lots may have been provided with individual connections to public utilities.

Subordinate Financing: Any lien against a parcel of real property which has lower priority than the first mortgage.

Sub-prime Mortgage: Prime mortgages are standard mortgages, conforming to underwriting requirements which fit borrowers with good credit and typical ratios for loan to value (LTV), and payments to gross income. Sub-prime mortgages, non-conforming loans or *creative* financing represent those mortgages targeted at buyers with poor credit scores, who do not generally qualify under standard underwriting requirements. They are considered much higher risk and generally bear higher interest rates.

Survey: The result of a surveyors measurements of the boundaries and other relevant characteristics of a parcel of real property, typically according to the property's legal description. Surveys may be required by the title company as a prerequisite for certain types of title insurance.

Sweat Equity: Work, labor or services performed on a property by a buyer in lieu of a cash contribution toward the value of the property's purchase price.

Tax Shelter: Any legal method by which one can avoid or at least reduce tax liabilities.

Tenancy by the Entirety: A joint tenancy of property that offers rights of survivorship and is available a legally married husband and wife. See "Tenancy in Common."

Tenancy in Common: A joint tenancy in a property without noted rights of survivorship. See "Tenancy by the Entirety and Joint Tenancy."

Tenant (Lessee): A tenant is one who holds or otherwise possess a property under the terms of a contract.

Termite Inspection: An inspection use to discover whether a property has termite damage or infestation. A home must be inspected for termites before it can be sold in many parts of the U.S.

Third-Party Origination: When a lender uses another party to completely or at least partially originate and otherwise process a mortgage. See "Mortgage Broker."

Time Value of Money (TVM): The concept that, even after inflation, the value of a dollar held now would be worth more than a dollar in the future because a dollar in possession now can earn interest, etc., until such time as a future dollar would be received.

Title: (1) A legal right to own (or a partial interest therein), possess, use, control, hold and dispose of real estate, and/or (2) any rights of ownership recognized and protected by law.

Title Insurance: A statement of fitness of the condition of a title describing the ownership of a real property. This insurance premium is paid, usually, with a one-time-only payment. Those so insured are protected against title defects, liens and other encumbrances.

Title Report: See "Abstract" or "Title Search."

Townhouse: A townhouse is a structure—usually of several stories—that shares a common wall or walls with similar structures.

Transfer of Ownership: The legal transfer of property from one owner to another.

Transfer Tax: When the title to a property passes from one owner to another, certain state or local taxes know as *transfer taxes* may be payable.

Treasury Index: Based on auctions of Treasury bills and securities by the U.S. Treasury, this index determines the interest rate for adjustable-rate mortgage (ARM) plans.

Triple Net Lease: In a triple net lease, a lessee pays rent, taxes and insurance, and maintenance costs to the lessor.

Trustee: See "Deed of Trust."

Trustee's Sale: Sale of a foreclosed property conducted by a trustee under the limits of a deed of trust. Upon default of a deed of trust, a designated trustee is authorized to foreclose on the mortgage and conduct trustee's sale the proceeds of which are distributed by the trustee as laid out in the deed of trust.

Truth-In-Lending Act (TILA): A Federal law that requires disclosure of a truth-in-lending statement which includes a summary of the total cost of credit.

Underwriting: The process of getting loan approved. It involves such things as evaluating property for which the loan is written as well as the credit worthiness of those taking out the loan.

VA Loan: A mortgage guaranteed by the U.S. Department of Veterans Affairs (VA).

Variance: Authorization to act contrary to a standing rule, for example, a zoning variance.

Veterans Affairs (VA): U.S. Department of Veterans Affairs. A Federal government agency that provides benefits to veterans and their dependents, including health care, educational assistance, financial assistance, and guaranteed home loans.

Waive: To voluntarily, knowingly or intentionally relinquish a granted right, claim or privilege.

Walk-Through: A clause commonly found in sales contracts that allow the buyer to examine the subject property at a specified time before the closing.

Warranty Deed: The deed used in many U.S. states that conveys fee title to real property.

Workout: A plan aimed at resolving indebtedness, such as those in lieu of a bankruptcy or foreclosure.

Wraparound Mortgage: A mortgage that holds the remaining balance on an existing first mortgage, plus an additional amount as requested by a mortgagor. The payments to both mortgages are made to the wraparound mortgagee, which are sent on to the first mortgage and the first mortgagee.

Yield: An annual rate of return on an investment, shown as a percentage.

Zoning: Local and state laws or rules governing the usage of property, such as residential (homes, for example) and commercial (businesses, industrial, etc.) property.

Source: Information provided by the Federal Trade Commission was used in preparing this glossary.

LaVergne, TN USA
22 January 2010
170907LV00002B/33/P